Health promotion and the community pharmacist

Health Education Authority
Hamilton House
Mabledon Place
London
WC1H 9TX

ISBN 1 85448 969 0

Typeset by Type Generation Ltd, London
Printed in England by BPC PAULTON BOOKS LTD.
A member of the British Printing Company Ltd.

CONTENTS

ACKNOWLEDGEMENTS

Thanks go to

- The Pharmacy Advisory Group and Mike Burden, for the initial idea

- Mary Allen and Fran Duggan, for the project proposal

- Mary Allen and Michelle Styles (NPA Information Department), for the majority of text

- Paula Hunt (HEA Primary Health Care Unit, Oxford)

- Sharon Whooley and Sonia Garner (NPA Information Department)

- Jane Todd (Barnet Health Promotion Centre)

- John Harris (Bexley Health Authority)

- Tim Astill (for encouragement and support)

- Ray Todd (NPA Pharmacy Planning Department)

FOREWORD

'Ask your pharmacist' is becoming a catchphrase. As a result of the advertising campaign which the National Pharmaceutical Association (NPA) began in 1982, more and more people have become accustomed to getting advice and information on health-related matters from their local community pharmacist. Pharmacies are readily accessible – there are almost 10,000 in NPA membership – and there is always a professionally qualified pharmacist present whenever the pharmacy is open. The pharmacist has not only a very detailed knowledge of the properties of medicines but also a broad training in pharmaceutical sciences and is an ideal 'filter' for those seeking help with family health problems and the treatment of common ailments.

But, like other health professionals, pharmacists have come to recognise the value of health education and disease prevention. The pharmacist is one of the only health professionals who regularly sees large numbers of healthy people and the pharmacy is therefore an ideal point from which to disseminate messages about healthy living, healthy eating, safer sex, smoking cessation, the safe use and storage of medicines and a whole range of other matters which will help to achieve the objectives laid down in *The health of the nation*. This book presents the results of a great deal of hard work by the NPA Information Department, funded by the Health Education Authority. Here is comprehensive guidance and a wealth of information for those pharmacists who believe that prevention is better than cure. There is at present an increasing interest amongst community pharmacists in health promotion: they are all interested in helping to improve the health of the nation and there are also some interesting changes being made to the pharmacists' NHS contract which will undoubtedly encourage them to use some or all of the material in this book. I know that it will be read with interest; I hope it will be widely used.

Tim Astill
Group Director
National Pharmaceutical Association

PREFACE

For centuries the practice of pharmacy has involved giving information and advice on ailments, their symptoms and their treatment. So is the recent emphasis on health promotion a new departure in the role of community pharmacists, or simply the new in-word for a traditional aspect of practice? A close review of the literature shows that neither of these assumptions is correct.

Health promotion in community pharmacy practice has been mentioned in the pharmaceutical press since the 1950s, although with increasing frequency since the Nuffield report[1] argued for an extended role for community pharmacists. More recently health promotion has gained in prominence because of the government's new health strategy, *The health of the nation*.[2] This is because the health strategy has identified certain behaviours, such as smoking, inappropriate diet and excessive alcohol intake, as constituting risk factors of the major causes of premature death. The main thrust of *The health of the nation* then is to promote healthy behaviours in order to combat the main causes of mortality in the population.

This focus on disease prevention provides the answer to the second assumption: that health promotion is not a new aspect of community pharmacy practice. The provision of medication may result in the effective treatment of a condition, and thus the clients' health will be improved. This act only constitutes health promotion however if there is a disease prevention element to it. So providing information and advice about a respiratory complaint, cystitis, nappy rash and a myriad of other minor ailments would be defined as health promotion only in so far as knowledge is imparted on how to prevent a re-occurrence. This is the crucial difference between disease management and health promotion. What does cause confusion however is that two terms, health promotion and health education, are used to describe these types of activity, and what is more, they seem to be used interchangeably. To throw light on the issue of what is meant precisely by these terms, we need to start with some definitions.

The World Health Organization's definitions are, by their nature, rather

3

general and unhelpful. The *Ottawa charter for health promotion* defined it more specifically in 1986.

> Health promotion is the process of enabling people to take greater control of their health to improve it. Its main elements are:
>
> - Creating supportive environments for health
> - Strengthening community action
> - Developing personal skills
> - Re-orienting health services
> - Building healthy public policy.[3]

More recently the Health Education Authority in its 1993–98 strategy statement provided a detailed explanation of the meaning of health education.

> Through health education, which is an essential instrument of health promotion, the public can gain knowledge, skills, motivation and confidence to pursue healthier ways of life; those who advise the public about their health can acquire the communication skills they need; decision makers in organisations can be advised on introducing health policies and on the health implications of other policies; and a climate of opinion can be created which supports comprehensive strategies to promote the health of the people. Health education is not something which only health educators do – everyone has a part to play.[4]

In essence the two statements refer to the same endeavour and so the two terms can be used interchangeably, although health education is the older term and historically has emphasised a purely educational approach. In practice health education has been largely superseded by the broader term health promotion.

The last part of the HEA's definition is less equivocal and that is that everyone has a part to play. This theme reinforces the challenge issued by Mrs Virginia Bottomley in her introduction to the government's health strategy: that *The health of the nation*'s targets are for all of us to achieve.

The purpose of this book is to assist you in playing your part in health promotion, by providing information, advice and references to sources of further assistance. It is based on the idea that, if advice and information is shared between pharmacists, consistency of message is guaranteed. This reinforces the advice which is presented to clients and prevents confusion due to mixed messages.

It is important not to underestimate the impact that the advice can have. Advice, information and counselling can raise awareness of health issues, promote understanding and reinforce the messages of local and national campaigns. Providing the right information at the right time in an appropriate way can help clients to change their lifestyles, circumstances and health for the better.

John Harris
Director of Health Promotion Services
Bexley Health Authority

References

1. *Pharmacy: a report to the Nuffield Foundation*, Nuffield Foundation, 1986.
2. *The health of the nation: a strategy for health in England*, Cm 1986. HMSO, 1992.
3. 'Ottowa charter for health promotion', WHO, Health and Welfare Canada, Canadian Public Health Association, November 1986. *Health Promotion* 4:1, 1987.
4. *HEA strategy 1993–98*. Health Education Authority, 1993.

1 The role of the pharmacist

There are six million visits made to pharmacists daily in the UK. This means the public has more contact with pharmacy than with all other healthcare professions put together. In addition, community pharmacists are unique within healthcare in seeing members of the public in health as well as in sickness. Pharmacists therefore have a very important role to play in the promotion of health and the prevention of disease.

The government has recognised the important role that pharmacists have in health promotion by including it as one of the requirements for payment of the new professional allowance.

There are various ways in which pharmacists can contribute to health promotion:

- Setting aside an area for consultation and health promotion
- Providing health promotion literature
- Using window displays to feature health promotion messages
- Counselling and advice
- Showing in-store videos or providing a video loan service
- Talks to local interest groups
- Health screening
- Providing other services.

We will look at each of these topics in detail.

Setting aside consultation areas

The size of your consultation area will depend on the services you offer and on the size of your pharmacy. Some pharmacists prefer to provide a room for this purpose, but there is a growing consensus among both pharmacists and customers that a designated area is more appropriate than a separate room.

A consultation area provides space for the pharmacist and customer to talk discreetly about matters relating to illness, or medicines, or for health promotion advice. The area can also be used to bring together all the services and merchandise relating to healthcare, and in most pharmacies is best placed to the side of the medicines counter or dispensary.

The following could be featured in the healthcare area:

- Health information leaflets from an appropriate stand
- Blood-pressure monitoring machine and stool
- Weighing machine
- Books on health topics for sale
- Healthcare videos (for viewing or for sale)
- Notice board informing customers of the services provided by the pharmacy
- Posters.

Note that testing involving body fluids must be carried out in a separate area.

Depending on the size of your pharmacy, you may wish to use the consultation area for giving prescription medicines, so that suitable advice can be given discreetly.

The diagrams on pages 9 and 10 show two suitable layouts for the consultation area in relation to the dispensary and medicines counter.

Notes

1. Where possible, avoid taking customers into the dispensary. Only do this as a last resort when the visitor is personally known to the pharmacist.
2. Set procedures should be agreed in advance with the staff, when customers request a consultation. It may be useful to introduce an appointments system or set aside a particular afternoon for certain topics of consultation, for instance blood-pressure monitoring.
3. A notice board in the consultation area provides a useful way of communicating the services on offer in the pharmacy. Removable plastic letters, which come in alphabet sets, allow flexibility so that

Consultation area 1 : key

1. Information panel
2. Health promotion and practice leaflets
3. Blood-pressure monitoring equipment
4. Seat
5. Consultation counter and handing out of prescribed medicines
6. Till point
7. Medical counter
8. Original pack dispensing
9. Wet bench

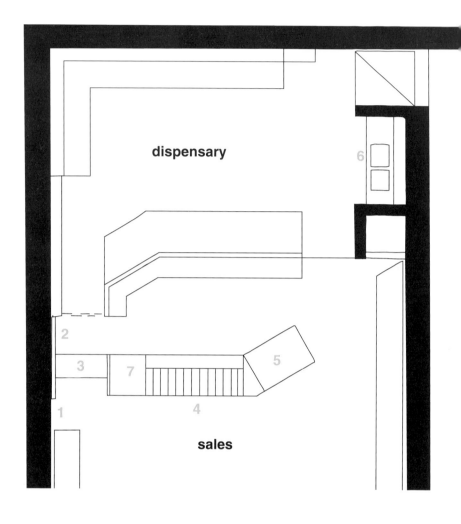

Consultation area 2 : key

1. Information panel
2. Health promotion and practice leaflets
3. Consultation counter
4. Medical counter
5. Till point
6. Wet bench
7. Glazed or plain screen for adding privacy

additional messages can be introduced occasionally. Some wholesalers provide other information aids.

4. Practice leaflets can be displayed alongside health information leaflets, so that customers can be made aware of the services you offer.

5. Notices, leaflets and booklets can quickly become eyesores if they are not regularly checked and updated. Leaflets and booklets for free distribution must be kept separate from items which are for sale. All booklets and leaflets are best displayed in properly designed racks or stands – see page 13.

6. Simple techniques such as the use of loose drapes can be used to 'soften' the professional area. This is particularly useful if the area is to be used for counselling.

Full advice on planning a consultation area can be obtained from the Pharmacy Planning Department of the National Pharmaceutical Association, tel: 0727 832161.

Providing health promotion literature

Leaflets

The provision of leaflets should be undertaken by all pharmacies, even if no other health promotion services are provided.

Leaflets on health promotion are included under seven main topics in Chapter 3. General sources of supply are given in Chapter 4.

Number of leaflets on display

One of the requirements for payment of the new 'professional allowance' is that you display leaflets on health promotion. Your family health services authority (FHSA) will advise you on the number of different leaflets you need to display. (The Department of Health requires FHSAs to determine the number, up to a maximum of eight, in consultation with local pharmaceutical committees.)

You may of course keep more than this number, but you need not display all your leaflets at once; often it is more effective to select an appropriate leaflet for your customer from a stock in the dispensary to reinforce the verbal advice you give.

You should monitor the number and range of leaflets on display to maximise their effectiveness and impact. Make sure that the display stand is well stocked and neat and that the leaflets are relevant and current.

In some circumstances, it may be appropriate to display posters relating to the leaflets stocked, to promote, for example, national campaigns. (See Appendix for important dates in 1994.)

Effective use of leaflets

You should ensure that you use the leaflets actively to reinforce health messages, rather than just leaving them on display for your customers to pick up. For example, selling a cough mixture to someone with an obvious smoker's cough provides an opportunity to introduce the subject of smoking cessation.

You can also personalise leaflets for your customers, for example, by writing on personal medication details. You should also be selective about which leaflets and how many you give to each customer – more is rarely better!

Displaying leaflets

You may have a section of your pharmacy set aside for the provision of health promotion where you can display your leaflets. However, in some cases it may be more appropriate to display certain leaflets in other areas of your pharmacy. For example, you could display leaflets on skin cancer or holiday health near the suntan preparations and leaflets on safer sex near the condoms.

Quality assurance

Many health promotion units check leaflets to ensure they are suitable for the intended market, in terms of readability, accuracy and bias. You should make sure that you check any leaflets you receive from other sources for accuracy and bias to ensure that you are putting across the right messages.

Remember, by giving out a leaflet, you are personally endorsing the information contained in it, so make sure you agree with what it says.

Where there are a large number of high quality leaflets available, you should not display only manufacturers' leaflets due to their inherent bias.

Special needs

You should try to provide leaflets to address the needs of people with special needs where possible. For example, leaflets with large print are available from health promotion units on topics of relevance to older people.

Ethnic minority communities

Some leaflets have been translated into other languages and it would be appropriate to use these where relevant.

Leaflet stands

All pharmacies receive leaflets every few weeks from the Pharmacy Healthcare Scheme and all pharmacies have received stands in which to display the leaflets from the scheme.

There are other stands available to allow greater flexibility of display. Large pharmacies will wish to use large stands to provide a wide range of leaflets while smaller pharmacies may require smaller, free standing units to use on a counter top.

Some FHSAs are now funding the purchase of leaflet stands for pharmacies so you could explore this possibility.

Suppliers of stands

- NPA Business Services

   Four stands are available.

   Spinner stand: polycoated wire. Takes 27 x ⅓ A4 and 6 x A5 leaflets. The stand measures 66" high x 16" diameter. It comes with three header cards and costs £39. Ref: LSS001.

Wall frame: polycoated wire. Optimises the use of unoccupied wall space and pillars. Takes 9 x ⅓ A4 and 2 x A5 leaflets. Measures 37" high x 12" wide, and is supplied with a header card. Price £15.99. Ref: LWF001.

Counter dispensers: Two sizes: high quality, heavy duty acrylic counter-top leaflet dispensers. Price £7.10. Ref: LCD004 (four bay ⅓ A4).

More details available on request from NPA Sales Office, tel: 0727 832161.

Other suppliers of stands

- The Patient Support Trust

  Provides a wall-mounted display unit costing approximately £69 plus delivery. Contact the Patient Support Trust, tel: 0489 891482.

  The company also provides a supply of leaflets for the stand, charging an administration fee and postage.

- Pharmaceutical wholesalers

  Some wholesalers supply leaflet stands. Check with your wholesalers' lists.

Using window displays

Don't forget that windows can provide display areas for health promotion. Instead of opting for the 'one-of-everything' approach favoured by many pharmacies, you can use window displays to communicate health messages.

Pick a theme such as 'Smoking cessation' or 'Sunscreens' and combine leaflets, posters and products to produce an eye-catching display.

Why not ask local children to participate in a poster competition? You could display the best entries in your window.

Try to co-ordinate window displays with national campaigns such as 'No Smoking Day' and with other in-store displays and promotions. Health promotion days for 1994 are listed in the Appendix.

Make sure that you change your window display regularly to avoid it looking stale and tired and to make sure that it is relevant and up to date.

Counselling and advice

Pharmacists can advise on areas of health promotion as diverse as smoking cessation, diet and accident prevention. This advice may be pro-active as part of a particular campaign or may be reactive as a response to a particular request. For more information on individual topics, see Chapter 3.

Showing in-store videos or providing a video loan service

Video is a very important visual medium for getting your health promotion message across and, if you have room in your pharmacy, you may wish to show videos on health topics. However, showing a video in your pharmacy may be illegal. The owner of copyright in a film has the exclusive right to permit or prohibit the public performance of his or her work. Anyone showing a video in public without the copyright owner's consent faces possible prosecution. Always obtain the copyright owner's permission, in writing, before showing in-store videos.

You should also bear in mind that customers can receive inappropriate messages from casual or partial viewing of a video (for instance if the video is viewed out of context). For example, a customer might see only snippets of a video whilst waiting for a prescription.

Therefore, it would not be appropriate for you to show a video which begins by presenting myths and debunks them later, or which shows bad practice which is later corrected, because there is no guarantee that the customer will receive the whole message. It may be more appropriate to show videos which are intended for use in GP or hospital clinics which are more likely to feature information in manageable bite-sized chunks.

It is essential that you preview all videos prior to showing them in your pharmacy to check the accuracy and appropriateness of either overt or covert advertising and to make sure that they are conveying clear and direct messages which you, as a pharmacist, can endorse. Remember, by showing videos, you are personally endorsing the information contained in them, so make sure that you agree with what they say.

Although you may show videos in the pharmacy, you're more likely to provide a loan or purchase service for customers so that they can view the videos at home. Again, ensure that the video is conveying the messages that you want to endorse.

Videos available on health promotion topics are listed on pages 78–83. Make sure that you have obtained the copyright owner's permission before showing any of these videos in your pharmacy.

Giving talks to local interest groups

Many pharmacists already provide talks to schools, parents and 'interest groups', such as self-help groups, on a wide range of health promotion topics. The National Pharmaceutical Association and the Royal Pharmaceutical Society send out regular press releases on health topics resulting in pharmacists participating in local radio interviews and so on. These are usually designed to coincide with national campaigns.

Contact local schools, women's groups, special interest and self-help groups to give talks on health promotion matters such as:

- Safe use of medicines
- Safer sex and sexual health
- Coronary heart disease prevention

- Smoking cessation

- Health of pregnant women and children

- Holiday health

- The menopause

- Prevention of head lice

- Drug use

- Health promotion for older people: healthy eating; keeping warm in winter; medicine storage/disposal; exercise.

Try to co-ordinate your talks with a window display in your pharmacy and any other in-store promotions or displays, or with national campaigns.

Make sure that you have prepared your talk well beforehand – use the resources of your local health promotion unit if necessary.

The National Pharmaceutical Association Press Office, the Royal Pharmaceutical Society and a variety of other suppliers can provide talk-notes and audio-visual material suitable for using when giving talks. (See page 75.)

Make sure that you have practised your talk well in advance so that you can estimate how long it will take and so that you can anticipate any questions that might follow.

Some areas have Voluntary Services Councils which co-ordinate voluntary groups locally. Some are prepared to pay for lectures from pharmacists on relevant topics.

Health screening

Pharmacists can provide health screening services such as blood-pressure monitoring and blood cholesterol monitoring, including advice and referral where necessary. In some cases this will be 'results only' tests undertaken on behalf of GPs. Increasingly, diagnostic test kits and health monitoring equipment are becoming available over the counter for home use (for example, pregnancy testing kits). It is important that advice be given when these are sold, not just on their use but on the interpretation of results and what action should be taken once the result is obtained.

Remember that testing of body fluids should not be carried out in your counselling area or in the dispensary or in any area where food or drink is consumed.

You should make sure that you are following the guidelines laid down by the Royal Pharmaceutical Society on health screening, particularly those on testing body fluids, pregnancy testing in pharmacies and the guidelines on blood pressure measurement in the pharmacy. These guidelines cover the suitability of premises, quality assurance etc. and are laid out in the publication *Medicines, ethics and practice – a guide for pharmacists* which is sent free to every community pharmacist twice a year.

You should ensure that any equipment used for health screening is properly calibrated and is in good working order. You should arrange for your equipment to be checked regularly and you must participate in a quality assurance programme.

It is also a good idea to contact your local GPs to tell them that you will be offering a health screening service in your pharmacy and to agree local guidelines on patient referral, advice given, etc.

Patient counselling

When you undertake health screening in your pharmacy, you will need to counsel patients about the results of their test. The best time to do this is *before you perform the test*, when the patient will be more receptive to your health promotion messages. Any health promotion messages delivered after the test result has been obtained are less likely to be effective either because the patient will be relieved that the result is 'normal' or because he or she will be anxious because it is 'abnormal'.

You should also stress that results of a particular test (for instance cholesterol measurement) should not be taken in isolation because the patient may have other risk factors. If you believe that the patient is not at risk (for example, if they have no risk factors), then you should say so and offer him or her the option of not having the test.

You should also try to give the patient a relevant leaflet so that they can remember what you have told them verbally.

Confidentiality

You should ensure that all information provided by the patient and the results of tests are kept confidential and are only disclosed to the patient and GP with permission.

Patient referral

You should provide patients with a written result of their screening tests. Some of the companies that supply equipment (for example pregnancy testing kits for professional use) can supply suitable forms, or the National Pharmaceutical Association can supply patient referral forms in the form of a duplicate book.

Where the patient's results are not within the desirable range, a copy of the form should be sent to the patient's GP (with his or her permission).

Suggestions for health screening in the pharmacy

- Blood pressure monitoring
- Body mass index calculation
- Cholesterol measurement
- Pregnancy testing (you could also carry out urinalysis to check for proteinuria, glycosuria, etc. as part of this service)
- Diabetes screening
- Asthma monitoring (peak flow monitoring).

Suppliers of equipment for health screening are given on pages 85– 97.

Note that the Health Education Authority does not support home or self-testing of cholesterol levels (see page 27).

Providing other services

A pharmacist is often the first amongst healthcare professions to see a prospective patient and can refer him or her to other professionals for advice so that potential illness can be avoided, or treated at an early stage. The National Pharmaceutical Association provides patient referral forms at reasonable cost for this purpose. Eventually referral forms may be supplied free of charge to pharmacists via FHSAs.

Many pharmacists are joining in syringe and needle exchange schemes for injecting drug users, to minimise the spread of diseases such as HIV and hepatitis B from shared contaminated needles. As well as promoting health through harm reduction, this service provides an opportunity to address other areas of health promotion such as safer sex.

Pharmacists can promote better use of medicines and can give advice on their storage in the home. In this way, and by receiving unwanted medicines from the public for disposal, pharmacists can reduce the number of accidental poisonings in the home.

2 Improving your health promotion services

By liaising with other healthcare professionals you can provide support for their activities, or use them to support your activities. The value of collaboration with other primary care and health promotion workers cannot be stressed too greatly, and will help to ensure that health promotion messages are consistent across the whole area or district.

There is a 'Health promotion contacts' chart on pages 104–5 which you can use to record the details of the following useful health professionals.

The local health promotion officer

Find out who yours is! He or she will usually be employed by the district health authority or trust, or may be attached to the local authority environmental health department. Find out if there is a local health promotion unit and pay a visit. Health promotion units are often a useful source of health information leaflets and other resources (such as displays, videos, posters), training courses and advice on health promotion issues. You should be able to locate your health promotion officer through the local telephone directory, or by contacting the district health authority or the environmental health department of the local authority. Failing this the Health Education Authority should be able to help (tel: 071 383 3833).

FHSA health promotion facilitator

Family health services authorities are now starting to co-ordinate health promotion activities in primary care. The person responsible within each FHSA may have one of various titles. In some FHSAs the work will be undertaken by the health promotion facilitator, who will co-ordinate health promotion across primary care (although, in practice, this currently usually relates to GP practice). In some FHSAs, the pharmaceutical adviser may have responsibility for health promotion in pharmacies.

Find out who is responsible for health promotion through pharmacies at your FHSA and contact them.

If there is no one at the FHSA with responsibility for health promotion in pharmacies make sure you change this, either directly or via your local pharmaceutical committee.

Work with your FHSA health promotion contact to co-ordinate health promotion activities throughout pharmacies in the area.

Some FHSAs now offer training in health promotion for community pharmacists and provide accreditation to those who participate.

General practitioner and practice nurse

Contact the local GP practices to let them know about your health promotion activities, particularly if you provide health screening or offer particular specialist advice, for example on smoking cessation, travel advice or advice to patients with particular problems, such as diabetes or stoma.

Dietitian

There is at least one dietitian in each district health authority or trust. Make contact with yours through the community unit or your main local hospital – he or she may be able to provide leaflets and other advice. If you offer, for example, a cholesterol screening service, it is important to check that you are giving consistent advice.

Health visitor

Work with health visitors to ensure consistency of advice relating to mothers and children. There are ample opportunities for liaising to convey health messages – pregnancy, breast-feeding and bottle-feeding, childhood immunisation and treatment of post-immunisation fever, head-lice, threadworms and childhood illnesses.

Community nurse

Let community, district and school nurses know how you can help with, for example, a co-ordinated approach to head-lice prevention, dental health, or sexual health/contraception (for older teenagers).

Dentists

Work together with dentists on prevention of dental caries, sugar-free medicines, fluoride, etc.

Environmental health officer

Liaise with the local environmental health officer (EHO) for a co-ordinated approach to publicity on the disposal of unwanted medicines. EHOs are often responsible for locally organised 'Home safety' weeks.

Local newspaper/radio

You could contact yours and provide, or contribute to, a regular feature on health promotion.

Funding for practice research or pilot schemes

There is some funding available for practice research or pilot schemes in the area of health promotion. Listed below are possible sources.

The Department of Health

The DH has an enterprise award for pharmacy practice research. Applications are considered annually each December.

Contact: Department of Health Pharmaceutical Division
Richmond House
7a Whitehall
London SW1A 2NS
Tel: 071 210 5753

The Health Education Authority

The DH allocates funding for health promotion through pharmacies and makes this funding available via the HEA. This money funds most of the Pharmacy Healthcare Scheme leaflets but there is a limited amount available for suitable health promotion topics in community pharmacies. (This book was funded in this way and other projects include a smoking cessation project in Liverpool, and an attitudinal survey on alcohol advice through pharmacies.) Applications should be made, via the Pharmacy Advisory Group, to the Health Education Authority.

Regional health authorities

Some regional health authorities will provide funding for health promotion pilots/research in community pharmacies. Sometimes this is available for pharmacy use, sometimes for multi-disciplinary use. If you have a good idea, let them know.

Family health services authorities

Increasingly, FHSAs are funding health promotion projects undertaken in pharmacies. The 'Barnet High Street Health Scheme' has paved the way by providing training for pharmacists in health promotion and accrediting those who complete the course. Other FHSAs are following suit.

NPA Health Education Foundation

This charitable foundation has limited funds available for promoting health education through community pharmacies. Applications should be made to the NPA.

3 Topics to get you started

There are many opportunities for pharmacists to get more involved in health promotion. The following pages set out a number of key issues which you may want to explore:

- Coronary heart disease
- Smoking
- Nutrition and diet
- Skin cancer
- Contraception
- HIV infection prevention
- Accident prevention.

The list isn't intended to be exhaustive, but you'll find advice on how to tackle the topics and ideas about how to find relevant resources. Your local initiatives may differ from those we have described – in which case you may need to do some additional work with your local contacts. New topics and issues will of course come up from time to time, and every effort will be made to ensure that follow-up information is made available to you.

Coronary heart disease

Coronary heart disease is the most common cause of death in England (26 per cent of all deaths in 1991). It also accounts for approximately 2.5 per cent of total NHS expenditure. The term coronary heart disease (CHD) covers conditions such as angina, heart attack, arrhythmias and heart failure.

What pharmacists need to know

- *The health of the nation* targets on CHD
- How to obtain background information on the risk factors for CHD
- How to promote healthier lifestyles
- How to identify those at risk from CHD
- Where to obtain resources on this topic

The health of the nation targets on CHD

1. To reduce the death rate for CHD in people under 65 by at least 40 per cent by the year 2000.

2. To reduce the death rate for CHD in people aged 65 to 74 by at least 30 per cent by the year 2000.

The major risk factors for CHD are smoking, hypertension, raised plasma cholesterol and inadequate exercise. Other risk factors include obesity, excessive alcohol intake and inadequate nutrition. Smoking and nutrition are dealt with in separate sections. *The health of the nation* targets for the other risk factors are described below.

The health of the nation CHD risk factor targets

Obesity

- To reduce the percentage of men and women aged 16–64 who are obese by at least 25 per cent for men and at least 33 per cent for women by 2005.

Blood pressure

- To reduce mean systolic pressure in adults by at least 5mm Hg by 2005.

Alcohol

- To reduce the proportion of men drinking more than 21 units of alcohol per week from 28 per cent in 1990 to 18 per cent by 2005 and the proportion of women drinking more than 14 units per week from 11 per cent in 1990 to 7 per cent by 2005.

Information/training needs

General health promotion

The Centre for Pharmacy Postgraduate Education (CPPE) provides a distance-learning pack, *Health promotion and health screening,* which contains general background information on health promotion as well as some useful chapters on screening for CHD risk factors.
Tel: 061 275 2324

A booklet *Better living, better life* (£15), intended for members of the primary healthcare team, looks at ways of preventing CHD through healthy lifestyles.
Available from Knowledge House Ltd, 13 Fairmile, Henley-on-Thames, Oxon, RG9 2JR.

The health guide – helping you to a healthier lifestyle includes useful information on choices of food, exercise, drinking and smoking.
Health Education Authority
Tel: 071 383 3833

Cholesterol testing

The HEA considers that testing of cholesterol levels should only be undertaken as part of an overall assessment of the risk for coronary heart disease when other risk factors (such as smoking, hypertension, family history, physical activity) are present. This is because the level of cholesterol alone is insufficient to predict CHD risk with confidence. Testing should ideally be carried out by a health professional who is able to take a good clinical history and identify other CHD risk factors; to apply a reliable testing procedure; and to give advice, counselling and follow-up for those with raised cholesterol levels. Self testing is not recommended.

The NPA's booklet, *Cholesterol screening and community pharmacy* contains useful information on setting up a cholesterol testing service. This is available free to NPA members or at a cost of £5 to non-members. Tel: 0727 832161

The Royal Pharmaceutical Society has two videos, *Cholesterol measurement in community pharmacy* and *Blood cholesterol and its monitoring*, which are available free on loan from the audio-visual service. Tel: 071 735 9141

Alcohol intake

The HEA publishes a pack for health professionals to help patients reduce their alcohol intake. The pack, *Cut down on your drinking*, includes guidance notes, patient's booklets and a poster. Tel: 071 383 3833

Hypertension

The Centre for Pharmacy Postgraduate Education (CPPE) provides a distance learning pack, *Hypertension*, which contains useful information on the role of hypertension in CHD and case studies on hypertension. Tel: 061 275 2324

What pharmacists can do

Provide health education material on CHD and its risk factors

- Display posters in your pharmacy about the risk factors for CHD.

Resources – posters

Posters are available from:
Health Education Authority
Tel: 071 383 3833

- Have leaflets on display about CHD and its risk factors.

Resources – leaflets

General

Are you or your family at risk?
Pharmacy Healthcare Scheme
A leaflet to educate the public about the risk factors associated with CHD and stroke.
Tel: 071 735 9141

You and your heart
Coronary Prevention Group
A leaflet on how the heart works, what heart disease is and how to avoid it.
Tel: 071 626 4844

British Heart Foundation
Supply a range of 30 leaflets free of charge.
Contact the publications department for an order form.
Tel: 071 935 0185

Alcohol awareness

That's the limit
Health Education Authority
About the effects of drinking, and advice on sensible drinking levels.
Tel: 071 383 3833

Exercise

Getting active, feeling good
Health Education Authority
Tel: 071 383 3833

Hypertension

Reducing blood pressure
Quaker Oats Nutrition Centre
Available free of charge.
Department NC 2207, Winterhill, Milton Keynes, MK6 1HQ

Blood pressure
Flora Project for Heart Disease
Available free of charge.
Tel: 0787 312196

Cholesterol

Blood cholesterol and your heart
Coronary Prevention Group
What blood cholesterol levels mean and what to do about them.
Tel: 071 626 4844

Dietary advice to lower blood cholesterol
Quaker Oats Nutrition Centre
Available free of charge.
Department NC 2207, Winterhill, Milton Keynes, MK6 1HQ

A range of cholesterol-lowering diet sheets, available in English
and in five Asian languages.
Bristol Myers Squibb
Tel: 081 572 7422

- Leaflets, posters and other educational material are also available
  from some food manufacturers. These usually emphasise the
  importance of diet, but also contain useful information on other
  risk factors. Suppliers include:

St Ivel Nutrition Department
Tel: 0793 848444

Flora Project for Heart Disease
Tel: 0787 312196

National Dairy Council
Tel: 071 499 7822

- Offer your customers tests for CHD risk factors. When you
  undertake health screening in your pharmacy, counsel patients before
  performing the test, when they will be more receptive to your health
  promotion message. If the patient has no risk factors for CHD you

could offer them the option of not having the test done because they are at low risk. You could also use your screening service to monitor those with existing CHD, for example patients recovering from a heart attack. You could offer to:

- **Carry out blood pressure measurement.** Suppliers of sphygmomanometers to measure blood pressure are listed on pages 96–7.

  A video to teach the techniques involved in blood pressure measurement is available from the British Medical Association (£24.95).
  Tel: 071 387 4499

- **Carry out cholesterol testing for customers who may be at risk.** Suppliers of cholesterol testing machines are listed on pages 85–6.

  A booklet is available from the NPA which gives detailed information on how to set up a cholesterol screening service in your pharmacy. It is available free of charge to NPA members or price £5 to non-members.
  Tel: 0727 832161

- **Carry out assessment of obesity using body mass index (BMI) calculations.** This is a simple measurement of the ratio of weight in kilograms to height in metres squared. Patients with a BMI greater than 27.5 are considered overweight and those with a BMI greater than 40 are considered obese.

  The widely used 'Garrow' chart showing healthy weight range based on BMI is available from the HEA.
  Tel: 071 383 3833

  Suppliers of weighing machines are listed on page 85.

- **Assess patients' physical fitness with a pulse or heart rate monitor.** Suppliers of these monitors are listed on page 96.

- **Organise a 'Pharmacheck' service, through a company called Pharmaforce.** The company provides a pharmacist to undertake cholesterol screening in your pharmacy and shares the profits with you.
  Tel: 0257 232518

● If you have room, show videos on CHD and its risk factors. This could be done while patients are awaiting the results of tests.

Resources – videos

Coronary artery disease – reducing the risk
NPA Press Office
Available free on loan to NPA members.
Tel: 0727 832161

Exercise your heart
Astra Pharmaceuticals
Supplied through pharmacies on request.
Tel: 0923 266191

Video on alcohol awareness
RPSGB Audio-visual Loan Service
Tel: 071 735 9141

A range of videos (some loaned free and some for a payment of £5 donation).
British Heart Foundation
Tel: 071 935 0185

Identify those at risk

You need to be able to identify which customers have risk factors for CHD so that you can target them with your health promotion message.

● If you carry out a health screening service (for example cholesterol screening, blood pressure measurement or body mass index assessment), you will be able to identify patients with risk factors and you will have the opportunity to counsel them on their lifestyle before or after giving them the result.

● When patients with prescriptions for antihypertensive, lipid-lowering medication, etc. come into your pharmacy, why not use it as an opportunity to discuss health promotion and give them a leaflet on the other risk factors for CHD?

● Patients requesting OTC medicines such as 75 mg aspirin tablets or cod liver oil capsules may be worried about CHD and may welcome the opportunity to discuss CHD prevention. You could display your leaflets near the food supplements section in the pharmacy.

● If you keep patient medication records you may be able to identify patients with risk factors and those recovering from heart attacks in this way.

Other ideas

● Get together with your local GPs, dietitians or practice nurses and run a coronary heart disease 'roadshow' in a local factory or other workplace or in a local child health clinic.

● Make sure that your customers know you can provide a health screening service as well as counselling and advice on minimising the risk factors for CHD. You could include a statement to this effect in your practice leaflet.

● Let local voluntary groups (for example your local branch of the British Cardiac Patients Association or Alcoholics Anonymous) know that you provide health screening services. You could offer to give a talk to the group.

● Keep a list of local self-help groups for those recovering from heart attacks and those suffering from coronary heart disease. Make sure that your customers know that they can use your pharmacy as a resource.

● You could offer to give talks on the risks of CHD to local schools as part of their programme of health education. CHD begins in childhood and so it is a good idea to target the young. Flipcharts of risk factors for heart disease which would be suitable for giving talks are available from the Flora Project for Heart Disease. Tel: 0787 312196

● 'Heart disease' might make an interesting project for younger children. Suggest it to one of the teachers and offer to judge a poster competition.

● Think about other ways of contacting young people, especially teenagers. Guides, Scouts, church groups and youth clubs may welcome talks on exercise, alcohol awareness, etc.

- Why not co-ordinate your activities around national or local campaigns such as national Drinkwise Day?

- Make sure that you (or the pharmacy's first-aider) have had adequate first-aid training so that you can perform basic resuscitation techniques if necessary. You will not always be able to prevent someone having a heart attack, but you may be able to save a life.

Useful contacts

Health Education Authority
Hamilton House
Mabledon Place
London WC1H 9TX
Tel: 071 383 3833

Coronary Prevention Group
Plantation House
31–35 Fenchurch Street
London EC3M 3NN
Tel: 071 626 4844

British Heart Foundation
14 Fitzhardinge Street
London W1H 4DH
Tel: 071 935 0185

Sports Council
16 Upper Woburn Place
London WC1H 0QP
Tel: 071 388 1277
Advice on physical activity.

Look After Yourself Project Centre
Christ Church College
Canterbury
Kent CT1 1QU
Tel: 0227 455687
Advice on physical activity.

Alcoholics Anonymous
General Service Office
PO Box 1
Stonebow House
Stonebow
York YO1 2NJ
Tel: 0904 644026

Alcohol Concern
305 Gray's Inn Road
London WC1X 8QF
Tel: 081 833 3471

Smoking

Lung cancer kills around 33,000 people in England every year. Smoking is the major risk factor for lung cancer – approximately 80 per cent of lung cancer deaths are directly associated with smoking and several hundred more deaths are caused by passive smoking. In the UK, the annual cost of smoking to the NHS is around £500 million.

What pharmacists need to know

- *The health of the nation* targets on smoking and lung cancer
- How to obtain background information on smoking cessation
- How to provide health education on the harmful effects of smoking and passive smoking
- How to help smokers to stop smoking
- How to prevent people from starting to smoke
- Where to obtain resources on this topic

The health of the nation targets on smoking and lung cancer

1. To reduce the death rate for lung cancer by at least 30 per cent in men under 75 and by at least 15 per cent in women under 75 by the year 2010.
2. To reduce the prevalence of smoking in men and women over the age of 16 to no more than 20 per cent by the year 2000.
3. To reduce smoking prevalence among 11–15-year-olds to less than 6 per cent by 1994.

Information/training needs

Leaflets and clinic guides which are suitable for those who run smoking cessation clinics are available from Quit.
Tel: 071 487 2858

The Health Education Authority also provides information for health professionals.
Give your mouth a break
Fact sheets and information leaflets on the effects of smoking on the mouth.

Smoking – helping people to stop
A resource pack with videos to help pharmacists giving talks or running clinics.
Tel: 071 383 3833

Most of the manufacturers of nicotine replacement products (for example the nicotine patch) produce useful background information on the principles of smoking cessation for health professionals. They also have helpdesks which pharmacists can contact for further information.

Kabi Pharmacia (Nicorette patches and gum)
Tel: 0908 661101

Ciba Laboratories (Nicotinell patches)
Tel: 0403 272827

Marion Merrell Dow (Nicabate patches)
Tel: 081 848 3456

What pharmacists can do

Set a good example

The NHS committed itself to being virtually smoke-free by the end of May 1993. Why not apply this to your pharmacy and designate it a smoke-free zone? The Royal Pharmaceutical Society's code of ethics states that smoking must not take place 'in any area where medicines are dispensed, sold or supplied'.

The HEA publishes a booklet, *Smoking policies at work*, describing how to introduce a smoking policy in the workplace.
Tel: 071 383 3833

Provide health education on the harmful effects of smoking

- Display posters in your pharmacy about the harmful effects of smoking and passive smoking.

Resources – posters

Posters can be obtained from your local health promotion unit or the Health Education Authority
Tel: 071 383 3833

Cleanair
Available in English, or English plus one other language (choice of six Asian languages, French, Spanish and Gaelic)
Tel: 081 690 4649

Tar and nicotine yield of cigarettes (posters and leaflets)
Department of Health Stores
No. 2 Site
Heywood Stores
Manchester Road
Heywood
Lancs OL10 2PZ

● Have leaflets on display about the harmful effects of smoking.

Resources – leaflets

Passive smoking
Smoking: the facts
Thinking about stopping?
Stopping smoking made easier
Give your baby a head start
Health Education Authority
Tel: 071 383 3833

Smoking and your heart
British Heart Foundation
Tel: 071 935 0185

Smoking and lung cancer
Imperial Cancer Research Fund
Tel: 071 242 0200

Smoking and your heart
Coronary Prevention Group
Tel: 071 626 4844

Smoking
Flora Project Information Division
PO Box 1392, Sudbury, Suffolk CO10 6FS

Smoking and pregnancy
Which? way to quit smoking: a consumer guide
Quit and stay slim
Quit
Tel: 071 487 2858

Leaflets are also available from the manufacturers of nicotine replacement products – see page 37 for details.

● Demonstrate the harmful effects of smoking in a practical way.

Carry out peak flow measurement to illustrate impaired lung function in smokers. Peak flow meters are available from most wholesalers.

Perform carbon monoxide measurements. Smokerlyzer machines measure the amount of carbon monoxide in exhaled breath.

These are available from Bedfont Scientific Ltd.
Tel: 0634 375614

Many health promotion units will provide Smokerlyzers on free loan for limited periods.

Show how much tar is taken into the lungs with a cigarette tar measurement kit which 'smokes' cigarettes.

This is available from Griffin and George.
Tel: 0509 233344

● If you have room, show videos on the harmful effects of smoking. This could be done while patients are awaiting the results of tests.

Videos are available from the manufacturers of nicotine replacement products – see page 37 for details.

> ## Resource – video
>
> *Quit and win*
> Health Education Authority
>
> Tel: 071 383 3833

Identify smokers

You need to be able to identify smokers who come into your pharmacy so that you can target them with your health promotion message.

If a patient with a 'smoker's cough' comes in to purchase an expectorant, why not give him or her a leaflet on the harmful effects of smoking and suggest if he or she wants to stop, then you are available to offer help and advice.

If you carry out a pregnancy testing service, you may have the opportunity to counsel the patient on her smoking habits before or after giving her the result.

If you keep patient medication records you may be able to identify smokers this way.

Helping smokers to stop

- Stock a range of products to help smokers give up (for example nicotine replacement products).

- Back this up with stocks of leaflets for patients which will give help and advice on stopping smoking. See pages 38–9 for details of leaflets.

- Run a smoking cessation 'roadshow' in a local factory or other workplace or in a local child health clinic.

- Make sure your customers know that you can provide counselling and advice on smoking cessation. You could include a statement to this effect on your practice leaflet.

● Stock a range of 'relaxation tapes' to help smokers give up.

> ## Resources – tapes
>
> Some tapes are available free to patients from manufacturers of nicotine replacement products. Others, which you can sell to your customers, can be obtained from:
>
> Albert Smith Health Cassettes
> Tel: 0255 672031
>
> Aleph One Ltd
> Tel: 0223 811679
>
> Webucational
> Tel: 0202 887439

● Let local voluntary groups (such as Smokebusters, and Quit) know that you stock and give advice on the use of smoking cessation aids. You could offer to give a talk to the group.

● There may be a stop-smoking group in your area to help smokers to give up. Contact your local health promotion unit for information.

Discourage people from starting to smoke

You could offer to give talks on the hazards of smoking to local schools as part of their programme of health education. You could bring along a peak flow meter or Smokerlyzer to illustrate the harmful effects of smoking as well as handing out some of your leaflets.

'Smoking hazards' might make an interesting project for younger children. Suggest it to one of the teachers and offer to judge a poster competition.

Think about other ways of contacting young people. Guides, Scouts, church groups and youth clubs, etc. may welcome talks on smoking.

Useful contacts

Health Education Authority
Hamilton House
Mabledon Place
London WC1H 9TX
Tel: 071 383 3833

Quit
102 Gloucester Place
London W1H 3DA
Tel: 071 487 2858

Action on Smoking and Health (ASH)
109 Gloucester Place
London W1H 3PH
Tel: 071 935 3519

Nutrition and diet

Dietary change in the whole population would contribute greatly to reduced morbidity and mortality from coronary heart disease (CHD), stroke and other chronic diseases. The current dietary recommendations for health may need to be modified for some groups, for example, children under five years, frail older people and women during pregnancy and lactation. Specific therapeutic dietary advice is also an important part of the management of many chronic and some acute disease states and in most cases requires the specialist advice of a state registered dietitian.

What pharmacists need to know

- *The health of the nation* targets on diet
- How to present nutrition and diet as a health promotion topic
- How to support people in dietary change
- How to identify people with dietary needs which differ from the general dietary recommendations
- How to differentiate between general dietary advice and specific therapeutic dietary advice, thus knowing when to refer people on to others
- How to access the specialist skills of state registered dietitians
- What other agencies can offer – for example, health professionals, sports and leisure facilities, support groups
- Where to obtain resources on this topic

The health of the nation dietary targets

The eating-related targets of *The health of the nation* strategy fall within the key target area of CHD and stroke. Achieving the targets will require considerable change in the diet of the whole population. The targets are:

1. To reduce the average percentage food energy derived by the population from saturated fatty acids by at least 35 per cent by 2005 (from 17 per cent in 1990 to no more than 11 per cent).

2. To reduce the average percentage of food energy derived by the population from total fat by at least 12 per cent by 2005 (from about 40 per cent in 1990 to no more than 35 per cent).

3. To reduce the percentages of men and women aged 16–64 who are obese by at least 25 per cent for men and at least 33 per cent for women by 2005 (from 8 per cent for men and 12 per cent for women in 1986/7 to no more than 6 per cent and 8 per cent respectively).

4. To reduce the mean systolic blood pressure in the adult population by at least 5 mm Hg by 2005.

What pharmacists can do

Respond to queries

The main dietary queries raised within the pharmacy include those on general healthy eating, vegetarian diets, weight management (weight loss, weight maintenance after weight loss and weight gain), CHD risk (raised lipids, raised blood pressure, family history) and high fibre diets for constipation. People may also ask about the need for vitamin and mineral supplementation. Supplementation is not, however, recommended for the whole population and you can more usefully give practical advice for healthy eating which will ensure that all vitamin and mineral requirements are met.

Give up-to-date advice, consistent with both the local dietetic and primary health care policies. The biggest barrier to adopting a healthier diet is the public perception that messages change and conflict. It is vital, therefore, that dietary advice from a pharmacist is consistent with mainstream dietetic and medical opinion. Seek further training (page 47) if you are unsure – or encourage people to seek further and more comprehensive advice, if necessary, by seeing their GP and asking for a referral to the dietitian or practice nurse.

Questions about diet from those whose needs are more specific are trickier to deal with. Examples include diet during pregnancy/lactation, dietary management of diabetes, feeding infants and children under five years of age and nutritional needs of frail older people. Go ahead if you are confident that your advice is accurate, up-to-date and appropriate for the individual concerned. Again referral to a dietitian, practice nurse, health visitor or specialist nurse (for example a diabetes specialist nurse) for further advice may well be necessary.

Areas of dietary advice that always require the specialist knowledge and skills of the state registered dietitian and/or doctor include potential food allergies or intolerance (for example gluten, lactose), concern about undernutrition or malnutrition, suspected eating disorders and therapeutic dietary advice which is part of the management of a disease (for example renal disease, liver disease, cancer).

Advise appropriately

Equipping yourself with accurate knowledge about nutrition and diet is vital, but developing the appropriate skills and considering the environment are equally important.

Remember to consider people's cultural, social and economic needs when giving advice and respect their need for privacy when discussing their eating habits with you.

The most helpful and practical way of giving dietary advice is to base it on foods (for example bread, fruit, vegetables) rather than nutrients (for example saturated fat, energy, vitamins). A 'food groups' approach, shown on page 46, will help to convey the concept of a healthy diet and will achieve the dietary goals for good health. The diagram shows the types of food people might eat within each of the four food groups, and the proportion from each group required for a healthy diet. People can get variety by regularly eating different foods from within each of the four groups – and by trying to limit the 'extras'. The government is presently developing this approach into a 'National Food Selection Guide' which will become a standard system for nutrition education. Ask your local dietitians to keep you updated on progress.

Display appropriate dietary information

Display healthy eating leaflets for people to pick up and have other leaflets available to back up any dietary advice you give. The quality of leaflets available varies; some are excellent and some are of dubious value. Caution

The healthy food selection guide
For adults and children over 5 years

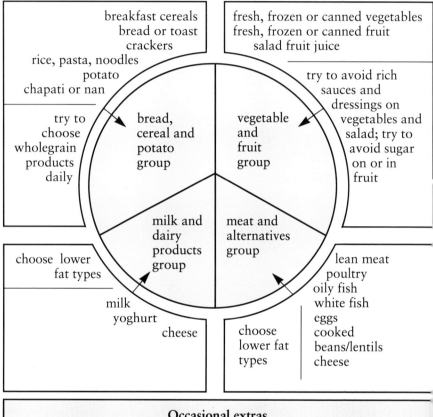

	Occasional extras	
fats (choose low fat types, or those made with unsaturated fat/oil)	low fat spread polyunsaturated margarine butter oil or cooking fats (lard, ghee) mayonnaise or oily salad dressing	try to limit to three servings daily
fatty and sugary foods	fatty meat, sausages, luncheon meat, crisps, biscuits, rich sauces, fatty gravies, cream, cream cheese, pastries, pies, cakes, doughnuts, chocolate rich/dairy ice cream	not essential but can add variety; should not replace foods from the 4 groups – try to limit to a maximum of once or twice daily

over the use of promotional leaflets from commercial sources is advised as their messages may be inconsistent.

Ask the local dietetic department to recommend suitable leaflets or approve those you wish to use. They may be able to supply their own to you at low cost.

Ensure all the resource or display material you offer (including posters and books) contains messages which are consistent with both the local dietetic and primary health care policies and with mainstream dietetic and medical opinion.

Know the referral system for state registered dietitians

Increasingly, dietitians are working in the community. State registered dietitians in your area may do regular clinics at the local health centre, surgery or hospital outpatients department where patients can be seen on a one-to-one basis. The professional code of conduct for dietitians previously required a medical referral for all patients seen for therapeutic dietary advice. However, this has recently changed and now makes the acceptance of referrals by other health professionals possible, providing an appropriate procedure has been set up which is agreed by dietitians and relevant medical staff. You can therefore suggest that patients make an appointment with their GP who can in turn refer them on to a dietitian, or discuss with appropriate dietetic and medical staff the possibility of setting up a direct referral system.

Information/training needs

Dietitians often offer regular nutrition training courses and workshops for primary care professionals. These may include technical updates on dietary aspects of health and disease, or skills based sessions, to offer participants an opportunity to develop their dietary counselling skills. Contact your local dietitian, or the health promotion unit or FHSA, for details of multi-disciplinary courses or ask if it is possible for the dietitians to set up a short course run specifically for pharmacists.

You may also find the following publications useful.

Nutrition and dietary advice in the pharmacy
Dr Pamela Mason
Copies available, at a discount to members, from the NPA, or contact the publishers, Blackwell Scientific Publications.
Tel: 0865 240201

Nutrition – a distance learning pack for community pharmacists
Centre for Pharmacy Postgraduate Education
Tel: 061 275 2324

Useful contacts

There is an abundance of public education material available but it can be of varying quality. Check with your local dietetic department if you are unsure about the appropriateness of any leaflet. In addition to your local dietetic service and health promotion unit (see pages 21 and 22 for how to contact them) you may also find the following helpful.

Health Education Authority
Hamilton House
Mabledon Place
London WC1H 9TX
Tel: 071 383 3833

The HEA publishes a range of nutrition resources.

HEA National Primary Health Care Unit
Churchill Hospital
Old Road
Oxford OX3 7LJ
Tel: 0865 226059

Ask for the nutrition/dietetic team for information and advice on nutrition in primary care.

British Dietetic Association
7th Floor
Elizabeth House
22 Suffolk Street
Queensway
Birmingham B1 1LS
Tel: 021 643 5483

Professional association representing state registered dietitians. Will provide contact details of your local nutrition and dietetic service in case of difficulty. The BDA also runs several members' special interest groups, which hold meetings and develop resources of possible relevance to pharmacists:

> Community Nutrition Group
> Paediatric Group
> Nutrition Advisory Group for Elderly People
> Mental Health Group
> Diabetes Management and Education Group

British Diabetic Association
10 Queen Anne Street
London W1M 0BD
Tel: 071 323 1531

Publishes many resources on dietary advice for diabetes and information updates for professionals – and a magazine, *Balance*.

Coronary Prevention Group
Plantation House
31–35 Fenchurch Street
London EC3M 3NN
Tel: 071 626 4844

Provides a good range of dietary information booklets and offers telephone advice.

National Dairy Council Nutrition Information Service
5–7 John Princes Street
London W1M 0AP
Tel: 071 499 7822

Has a mailing list for health professionals, and sends out *Nutrition update* and other professional and public educational materials.

St Ivel Nutrition Service
St Ivel House
Interface Business Park
Wootton Bassett
Swindon SN4 8QA
Tel: 0793 848444

Flora Project for Heart Disease
24–28 Bloomsbury Way
London WC1A 2PX
Tel: 071 242 0936

Meat and Livestock Commission
Nutrition Department
PO Box 44
Winterhill House
Snowdon Drive
Milton Keynes MK6 1AX
Tel: 0908 677577

Skin cancer

There are around 28,000 cases of skin cancer in England each year and about 1300 deaths. The incidence of skin cancer is rising and this is thought to be due to increased exposure to ultraviolet radiation (UVR).

There are two main types of skin cancer caused by the sun.

Malignant melanoma. This is a rare but dangerous form of skin cancer. It can spread rapidly, but if caught and treated early the chances of survival are good. Melanomas are commonest amongst sun-sensitive people who spend most of the year indoors and then take a holiday in the sun.

Non-melanoma. This form of skin cancer is far commoner than melanoma, and much less dangerous. It is nearly always curable. Non-melanomas are thought to be linked to long-term exposure to the sun, which is why people who work outdoors are at greater risk.

Pharmacists are well placed to provide advice on avoiding overexposure to UVR and consequent sunburn, since people often visit pharmacies for holiday requisites (including sunscreens).

What pharmacists need to know

- *The health of the nation* target on skin cancer
- What the risk factors for skin cancer are
- How excessive exposure to UVR can be avoided
- Where to obtain resources on this topic

The health of the nation target on skin cancer

To halt the increase in the incidence of skin cancer by the year 2005.

What pharmacists can do

Provide pharmacy-based health education on the harmful effects of the sun

Timing of a campaign on 'sun awareness' is crucial. It is probably best to run a campaign in late spring or early summer so that the health message is fresh in people's minds before exposure to the sun in the UK or overseas.

● Display posters in your pharmacy about the harmful effects of overexposure to the sun.

Resources – posters

Pharmacy Healthcare Scheme
Royal Pharmaceutical Society
Tel: 071 735 9141

Windsor Healthcare
Tel: 0344 484448

● Have leaflets available on different aspects of safe tanning. Display them near the sunscreens or sunglasses. Give them to people who come into your pharmacy to purchase holiday requisites, malaria tablets, etc.

Resources – leaflets

If you worship the sun don't sacrifice your skin
Health Education Authority
Tel: 071 383 3833

Smart cookies don't burn
Pharmacy Healthcare Scheme
Royal Pharmaceutical Society
Tel: 071 735 9141

Be a mole watcher for life
Cancer Research Campaign (£4 for 100)
Tel: 071 224 1333

Understanding malignant melanoma
BACUP (£1.50 each plus SAE)
Tel: 071 696 9003

Melanoma skin cancer fact sheet
Avoiding skin cancer
(Directed at outdoor workers)
Imperial Cancer Research Fund
Tel: 071 242 0200

Leaflets may also be available from the companies which manufacture sun lotions.

- If you have room, show videos on safe-tanning.

Resources – videos

Saving your skin
Pack includes video, accompanying booklet and leaflets for the public. £8.81.
Plymouth Medical Films
Tel: 0752 267711

Skin cancer teaching pack
Designed to teach schoolchildren how to prevent sunburn. Contains a video and teaching booklet. £7.50 plus VAT.
Imperial Cancer Research Fund PR Department
Tel: 071 242 0200

Provide advice on aspects of safe tanning

Make sure your customers know:

- **The HEA's advice on safety in the sun**

  - Avoid the midday sun but, if you do have to go out, cover up with loose clothing and a wide-brimmed hat.

  - Use sunscreens on your skin for protection – whichever is the right factor for you.

  - Tan slowly, gradually increasing the time you spend in the sun each day.

  - Young children should always be protected – either covered up or with a high-protection sunscreen.

  - Babies should never be allowed out when the sun is hot.

  - Don't burn. It doesn't protect against burning in the future. Burnt skin doesn't tan more quickly, just more painfully.

● **What their 'skin-type' and skin cancer risk is.** Make sure that parents know their children's 'skin-type'. A chart with this information is available from the NPA Information Department. Tel: 0727 832161.

● **The most appropriate suntan preparation for their needs** (for example try to dissuade fair-skinned people from buying lotions with a low sun protection factor (SPF)).

Other ideas

● Sunburn in early childhood is a very important risk factor for malignant melanoma. Offer to give talks to mother and toddler/women's guild groups, etc. You could also have a sun awareness 'roadshow' at the local child health clinic or a local summer fete.

● Offer to give talks to local schools, youth clubs, Brownie/Cub groups, Guide/Scout groups, etc. on this topic. The Imperial Cancer Research Fund can supply an information pack suitable for use in schools (see page 53 for details).

● 'Sun awareness' could make an interesting project for younger children. Suggest it to a local teacher and offer to judge a poster competition – you could display the best posters in your pharmacy!

● Why not have an eye-catching window display of suntan preparations, sunhats, buckets and spades, etc. to tie in with the campaign?

● Stock a wide range of sunhats for babies and adults. The NPA Information Department has details of suppliers. Tel: 0727 832161

● Some drugs, for example, chlorpromazine and the oral contraceptive pill, can cause photosensitivity. If you keep patient medication records you may be able to identify patients who are taking drugs which can cause photosensitivity and you can give them advice about buying appropriate sun protection. The NPA Information Department can provide advice on drugs that cause photosensitivity. Some sunscreen preparations are allowed on NHS prescription for photodermatoses (diseases of the skin caused by exposure to UV light) – contact the NPA Information Department for details. Tel: 0727 832161

● If you provide pharmaceutical services to residential or nursing homes, don't forget that residents are often put outside in summer to 'enjoy the sun' and may not be able to come back indoors by themselves – older people and people with disabilities can burn as well.

Useful contacts

Health Education Authority
Hamilton House
Mabledon Place
London WC1H 9TX
Tel: 071 383 3833

Cancer Research Campaign
10 Cambridge Terrace
London NW1 4JL
Tel: 071 224 1333

Imperial Cancer Research Fund
PO Box 123
Lincoln's Inn Fields
London WC2A 3PX
Tel: 071 242 0200

Contraception

Pharmacists are well placed to supply contraceptive products and to provide advice on family planning. The widespread distribution of pharmacies, long opening hours and the lack of need for appointments mean that many patients will approach a pharmacist for advice on contraception rather than using their GP or family planning clinic.

What pharmacists need to know

- *The health of the nation* targets on contraception
- How to help achieve these targets
- Where to obtain information about the different methods of contraception available
- What advice to give on emergency contraception
- How to present contraception as a health promotion topic
- Where to obtain resources

The health of the nation targets

1. To reduce the rate of conceptions amongst the under-16s by at least 50 per cent by the year 2000.

2. To ensure the provision of effective family planning services for those who want them.

Information/training

The contraceptive handbook which was sent free to all pharmacies in 1992 by the Pharmacy Healthcare Scheme provides useful background information. Additional copies are available from the Family Planning Association at a cost of £12.99. Tel: 071 636 7866.

Another useful reference source is the Centre for Pharmacy Postgraduate Education (CPPE) distance learning pack, *Women's health*. Contact your local CPPE tutor for details. You can find out who your local tutor is by contacting the CPPE. Tel: 061 275 2324.

Some of the companies who manufacture contraceptives can provide information about their use for health professionals.

Mates, a guide for family planning staff and their patients on the use of condoms is available free of charge from Sunderland Healthcare. Tel: 0635 874488.

What pharmacists can do

Provide pharmacy-based health promotion on contraception

- Display posters in your pharmacy about the effective methods of contraception.

Resources – posters

Family Planning Association
Tel: 071 636 7866

Durex Information Service
Tel: 081 527 2377

- Have leaflets available about the different methods of contraception.

Resources – leaflets

Your health, a guide to services for women
Department of Health
Tel: 0800 555777

Fourteen titles in English as well as books in Asian languages
Family Planning Association
Tel: 071 636 7866

Nine different titles. Up to 100 copies of each are provided free of charge; 5p per leaflet above that quantity.
Durex Information Service
Tel: 081 527 2377

Your guide to safer sex and the condom
Health Education Authority
Tel: 071 383 3833

Leaflets in five Asian languages as well as English
Wyeth Laboratories
Tel: 0628 604377

Conception and contraception
Schering Healthcare Ltd
Tel: 0444 232323

Women wise
Sanofi Winthrop Ltd
Tel: 0483 505515

Provide advice on other aspects of contraception

- Provide a pregnancy testing service in your pharmacy. Many young people will not be able to use a home pregnancy testing kit or may not 'trust' its accuracy. If you cannot provide a service, make sure that you offer advice to patients buying home testing kits, and recommend that they visit their doctor if the test is positive. This will require a considerable amount of tact and time and, where possible, should be carried out in a private consultation area.
  There is considerable scope for pharmacist intervention when carrying out pregnancy tests on young women. If the test is positive, they may need information on what their options are and where to go for advice. If negative, you can use it as an opportunity to provide information and advice on contraception for the future.
  For details of pregnancy testing kits available (home and professional use), see pages 88–93.

- Make sure you are able to provide accurate, up-to-date information on what a woman should do if she forgets to take her contraceptive pill.
  A 'missed pill calculator' is available free of charge to pharmacists from Cilag Ltd. Tel: 0494 563541.

- Many women approach pharmacists for advice on emergency contraception when doctors' surgeries are closed. Make sure that you are aware of the options available so that you can direct patients quickly to the most appropriate person for advice on emergency contraception. You may need to liaise with your local GPs and local family planning clinic to ensure that consistent advice is given. Some women believe that pharmacists can provide an emergency supply of the pills in case they are needed in the future. However, such supplies would not normally comply with Medicines Act requirements which state that the person must have been prescribed the medicine by a doctor before.

- Make sure that you only stock condoms that are marked with the British Standard 'kitemark' symbol. This guarantees that the condoms have passed stringent safety tests and so are more likely to provide effective contraception. There is no kitemark for the female condom but this does not necessarily mean its quality is reduced.

- Oil-based vaginal lubricants, ointments, creams and pessaries can damage the rubber of diaphragms or condoms. A leaflet listing those vaginal and rectal preparations which can cause damage to rubber and those which are safe to use is available from Durex Information Service. Tel: 081 527 2377.

  Remember that other medicines can interact with contraceptives (for instance some antibiotics can decrease the efficacy of the oral contraceptive pill).

- Have information available in your pharmacy about how to contact the family planning clinic in your area. This could take the form of a poster or leaflet displayed near the condoms. Ask your local family planning clinic if they have leaflets available or know where to get some.

- Make sure that your customers know you can provide advice on contraception and pregnancy testing. You could include a statement to this effect in your practice leaflet.

- Offer to gives talks to local schools, youth clubs and young people's groups on contraception as part of a programme on sex education. You could use the video *Contraception – know what you are doing*, available free on loan from the NPA Press Office (tel: 0727 832161). Bring along stocks of leaflets to hand out so that the young people can study them at leisure. It is best to contact your local health education unit for support and advice. They will be very helpful in getting you started and providing you with videos and other educational materials and contacts. They may also be running local sex education programmes in which you could participate.

Useful contacts

Family Planning Association
27–35 Mortimer Street
London W1N 7RJ
Tel: 071 636 7866

Brook Advisory Centres
153A East Street
London SE17 2SD
Tel: 071 708 1390
Advice on contraception and pregnancy counselling.

Catholic Marriage Advisory Council
Clitherow House
1 Blythe Mews
Blythe Road
London W14 0NW
Tel: 071 371 1341
Advice on 'natural' family planning.

Health Education Authority
Hamilton House
Mabledon Place
London WC1H 9TX
Tel: 071 383 3833

Margaret Pyke Centre
15 Bateman's Buildings
Soho Square
London W1V 5TW
Tel: 071 734 9351

Marie Stopes Clinic
Marie Stopes House
The Well Woman Centre
108 Whitfield Street
London W1P 6BE
Tel: 071 388 0662
Contraception and pregnancy counselling.

British Pregnancy Advisory Service
Austy Manor
Wooten Wawen
Solihull
West Midlands
B95 6BX
Tel: 0564 793225

HIV infection prevention

The Human Immunodeficiency Virus (HIV) represents one of the greatest health challenges this century. In the UK, HIV is primarily transmitted through unprotected sexual intercourse or sharing drug injecting equipment and pharmacists are able to provide advice on the prevention of HIV in these two main areas as well as other preventive advice.

What pharmacists need to know

- *The health of the nation* targets on HIV prevention
- How HIV is and is not transmitted
- Which methods of contraception provide an effective barrier to HIV
- How drug users can reduce the risk of contracting HIV
- How to present HIV infection prevention as a health promotion topic
- Where to obtain resources on this topic

The health of the nation targets

Note that *The health of the nation* did not set specific targets for HIV infection because it is not yet possible to establish baseline rates of incidence and prevalence against which to measure achievements.

However, *The health of the nation* does aim:

1. To reduce the incidence of HIV infection.

2. To reduce the percentage of injecting drug users who report sharing injecting equipment (20 per cent in 1990) to no more than 10 per cent by 1997 and no more than 5 per cent by the year 2000.

The health of the nation also states that local education and prevention work should aim to:

- improve levels of knowledge and awareness about HIV in the population

- help to encourage people to adopt healthy or safer patterns of sexual behaviour

- encourage people who may be at risk to modify and sustain changes in their sexual behaviour.

What pharmacists can do

- Use the section on contraception for health promotion information on contraception.

- Make sure that you stock condoms that are marked with the British Standard 'kitemark' symbol. This will guarantee that the condoms have passed stringent safety tests and so are less likely to tear and therefore increase the risk of HIV transmission.

- Stock condoms suitable for use for anal sex. This type of condom will be extra strong, lubricated and usually has no teat – for example, Red Stripe condoms (available through pharmaceutical wholesalers).

- Display notices or information in your pharmacy on local self-help and peer-based support groups. Details are available from the National AIDS Helpline (administration, tel: 071 387 6900) or your local drugs services.

- A leaflet listing preparations which can cause damage to rubber and those which are safe to use is available from Durex Information Service, tel: 081 527 2377. Copies could be displayed alongside your condom merchandising unit. Oil-based lubricants, for example Vaseline, can damage the rubber of condoms. This is particularly important if the condom is being used rectally or whenever extra lubrication is required.

- Consider participating in a syringe and needle exchange scheme in your area. Guidance can be obtained from the NPA information leaflet *Syringe and needle exchange* (available from the NPA on request). If you can encourage drug users not to share their needles or 'works', the risk of HIV transmission will be reduced. (If you are already operating an exchange scheme ensure that you follow the NPA model code of practice for safe operation.)

- Why not stock a range of sharps disposal boxes – for use in the scheme, or for sale to local surgeries, drug services, etc? (Details of suppliers are available from the NPA Information Department.)

- World AIDS Day occurs each year on 1 December. Arrange a promotion around this date and liaise with others to produce a local campaign.

- Offer to give talks to local schools, colleges or youth clubs on safer sex. It would be useful to have leaflets on the use of condoms and samples of condoms to hand out.

Resources

The HEA has a wide range of leaflets and posters on safer sex. Tel: 071 383 3833

You may also find AVERT's training pack *AIDS – working with young people* (£18.95) useful. Tel: 0403 210202

Barnardo's produce a leaflet which is suitable for secondary school children and their families. Tel: 081 550 8822

Provide other help and advice

- Stock a range of spillage kits for body fluids. These kits tend to include items such as absorbent granules, gloves, apron, disposal bag, and scoop, and are used by healthcare workers to clean up body fluid spillages (for example blood and urine, etc.). You could also stock mouth-to-mouth resuscitation aids. Details of suppliers can be obtained from the NPA Information Department.

- Customers travelling abroad may be concerned about the risk of HIV transmission should they require an injection or transfusion. Details on suppliers of travel kits (which generally contain syringes, needles, sutures, swabs, etc.) can be obtained from the NPA Information Department.

- Display information on local facilities for respite and terminal care for people with AIDS, such as:
  - local hospices
  - services provided by specialist nurses
  - outreach teams or 'buddy' support networks from local voluntary organisations.

- Find out the address and telephone number of your local genito-urinary medicine (GUM) clinic. You could display the details near your patient leaflets. The local GUM clinic is often a useful source of professional advice for people who think they may be at risk of HIV and are reluctant to contact their own GP.

- Display a list of HIV and AIDS helplines for people with varying communication needs:
  - Arabic. Tel: 0800 282447 (6–10 pm Weds)
  - Asian languages (Bengali, Gujarati, Hindi, Punjabi and Urdu). Tel: 0800 282445 (6–10 pm Weds)
  - Cantonese. Tel: 0800 282446 (6–10 pm Tues)
  - People who are deaf or hard of hearing. Tel: 0800 521361 (10 am–10 pm daily)

Useful contacts

See also 'Useful contacts' in contraception section.

Terrence Higgins Trust
52–54 Gray's Inn Road
London WC1X 8JU
Provides a range of services on HIV/AIDS advice centre, legal advice, counselling, drugs advice, safer sex advice, leaflets, posters.
Tel: 071 831 0330
Tel: 071 242 1010
(Helpline 12pm–10pm daily)

National AIDS Helpline
A 24-hour free and confidential service which will give information on local services.
Tel: 0800 567123 (Freephone)

Body Positive
51B Philbeach Gardens
London SW5 9EB
Tel: 071 835 1045
Provides general information, legal and health advice, newsletters, leaflets and posters.

Health Education Authority
Hamilton House
Mabledon Place
London WC1H 9TX
Tel: 071 383 3833

Accident prevention

Accidents are a major cause of avoidable illness, injury and death. They affect all age groups, but children, young adults and the elderly are particularly at risk.

What pharmacists need to know

- *The health of the nation* targets on accident prevention
- How pharmacists can prevent deaths due to accidents
- How to present accident prevention as a health promotion topic
- Where to obtain resources

The health of the nation targets on accident prevention

To reduce the death rate from accidents:

1. Among children under 15 years by at least 33 per cent by the year 2005.

2. Among young people aged 15–24 by at least 25 per cent by the year 2005.

3. Among people aged 65 and over by at least 33 per cent by the year 2005.

What pharmacists can do

Advice on the safe storage of medicines

- Make sure that your customers know how to store their medicines properly, out of the reach of small children and pets. Some parents may wish to buy lockable medicine cabinets or locks for ordinary cupboards and you can advise on the purchase of such items. Some medicines (for instance some antibiotic mixtures) should be stored in a refrigerator. Why not stock a supply of domestic refrigerator locks? The NPA Information Department can supply details on request. Tel: 0727 832161.

- Ensure that *all* solid-dose dispensed medicines are supplied with a child-resistant cap (CRC), where possible. (This has been a professional requirement of the Royal Pharmaceutical Society since January 1989.) Some elderly or arthritic people have difficulty in opening these closures; you may fit 'ordinary' caps, or even 'winged' caps to aid patient compliance, but make sure you counsel the patient to keep the medicine locked away safely if they have small children visiting. Remind patients that patient compliance devices, such as a Dosett or Nomad, are attractive to children. Child-resistant caps for liquid medicines are now available and it is likely to become a professional requirement of the Royal Pharmaceutical Society that they are used on all dispensed liquid medicines.

Resource – leaflet

A leaflet, *Medicines are not child's play,* is available from the Pharmacy Healthcare Scheme, Royal Pharmaceutical Society. Tel: 071 735 9141.

Advice on the safe disposal of unwanted medicines

Old and unwanted medicines should not be kept in the home where they might be used inappropriately or cause accidental poisoning. Encourage your patients to return old medicines to you for proper disposal. Make sure that they do not dispose of medicines with the household rubbish where they will end up on the corporation tip and could be consumed by a child.

Advice on the safe usage of medicines

- Make sure that patients know how to take their medicines properly to avoid accidental overdosage. When counselling patients, make sure that they understand how to take the medicine (for example, whether it is to be swallowed or applied to the skin) and remind them that medicines should not be shared with anyone else.

- Ensure that patients understand the dosage instructions on their medicines. For example, antibiotics should be taken until the course is finished, even though the patient may feel better. If the patient knows the importance of this, it will help prevent accumulation of unwanted medicines.

- Make sure that your patients understand the importance of any additional labels on their medicine. For example, some drugs can cause drowsiness and may affect the performance of tasks that require concentration. If any patient drives or operates machinery for a living, make sure that they know that drugs, including OTC medicines, can affect performance and cause accidents.

- Make sure that all your patients are aware of the importance of telling you about other medicines (including OTC medicines) that they might be taking.

> ### Resource – leaflet
>
> Copies of the leaflet, *How to take your medicine*, are available free of charge to NPA members from the NPA Press Office. Tel: 0727 832161

Advice on accidental poisoning

If someone has accidentally consumed a medicine or poisonous plant, or taken an overdosage, make sure you give appropriate advice on what action to take. Normally, the best course of action will be to refer the person to the nearest hospital accident and emergency (casualty) unit. A sample of the poison should be kept to show to the doctor.

> ### Resource – poster
>
> A poster on how to avoid poisoning accidents in the home is available from:
>
> Dr Alan Judd
> Leeds Poisons Information Service
> George Street
> Leeds LS1 3EY

Prevention of accidents in older people

● Many older people take drugs such as antihypertensives and diuretics which can cause postural hypotension, or drugs that can cause sedation. These can lead to an increased risk of falls. In addition, drug interactions can cause confusion. The extensive use of drugs by older people, coupled with the multiple disorders of old age, may cause serious complications. The medication of all older people (especially those living alone) should be reviewed regularly – why not suggest to your local GPs that you can help with a programme of medication review?

● Some older people have multiple drug regimes and cannot remember which drug to take when. If any of your older patients are confused, you could offer to dispense medicines into a patient compliance aid.

● Make sure that care assistants in residential homes or those who visit patients in their own home or in sheltered accommodation (for example, home helps) know how medicines should be used and how they should be administered. You should ensure that they have a safe and secure system or method of drug administration.

● Check that home care workers (such as home helps), community nurses, health visitors and anyone else who visits patients in their own home know about the safe storage of medicines.

Resources – training packs

For use by pharmacists training care assistants.

Take good care with medicines
Free from the Centre for Pharmacy Postgraduate Education. Contact your local CPPE tutor or telephone 061 275 2324.

Training for residential home care staff
Free (with video on loan) from the NPA Training Department. Tel: 0727 832161, ext 248

Care staff: understanding medicines
Available from the University of Brighton at a cost of £39.67 plus £1.50 p&p. Tel: 0273 642778. Can also be loaned from the Royal Pharmaceutical Society Audio-visual Service.Tel: 071 735 9141

● Why not stock a range of aids to daily living for older people and for people with disabilities? Some of these can be obtained from the major wholesalers; or contact the NPA Information Department.

Prevention of accidents in young people

Many young people are unaware of the behavioural changes caused by alcohol, drugs and solvents and their relation to increased risk-taking. Keep a stock of leaflets in your pharmacy about the dangers of drug or solvent use and about the safe use of alcohol. These can be picked up by young people or by concerned parents.

Resources – leaflets

Solvents – a parent's guide
Drugs – a parent's guide
Department of Health
Freepost, BS/4335
Bristol BS1 3YX
Tel: 0800 555777

What to do about solvent abuse
Re-Solv
Tel: 0785 817885

Solvent abuse and aerosols
Explains how solvent abusers misuse a variety of products and gives guidance on how to recognise a solvent abuser.
British Aerosol Manufacturers Association
Tel: 071 828 5111

Drug abuse at work
For employers who have an employee with a drug problem.
Health and Safety Executive
Tel: 0742 892346

OTC medicines abuse
Institute for the Study of Drug Dependence (95p each)
Tel: 071 430 1993

See the section on coronary heart disease for resources on sensible drinking.

Safe use of non-medicinal chemicals

Pharmacists often sell chemicals to small businesses or to members of the public for their own use. By law, some chemicals must be supplied with a child-resistant cap. It is unwise to break bulk unless you can comply with the packaging and labelling requirements. It is usually wiser to supply the manufacturer's original container.

Make sure that any chemicals sold are labelled properly. This should include a general indication of how the chemical should be used, together with any indications of the nature of the risks associated with the chemical (for example 'Causes burns') and any safety precautions to be observed (for instance 'Avoid contact with skin'). You should ensure that customers know how to use the chemicals properly.

If you sell chemicals to someone for use in their business then you should ensure that you pass on a safety hazard data sheet. This gives details of the risks involved in the use of the chemical together with information on what to do in an emergency situation. These can be obtained from suppliers of chemicals.

Information on packaging and labelling of hazardous chemicals can be obtained from the NPA Information Department.

Useful contacts

Health Education Authority
Hamilton House
Mabledon Place
London WC1H 9TX
Tel: 071 383 3833

Age Concern
Astral House
1268 London Road
London SW16 4ER
Tel: 081 679 8000
Supplies a range of free posters and leaflets for the public on accident prevention in older people.

Child Accident Prevention Trust
Fourth Floor
Clerks Court
18–20 Farringdon Lane
London EC1R 3AU
Tel: 071 608 3828
Runs Child Safety Week.

British Red Cross Society
9 Grosvenor Crescent
London SW1X 7EJ
Tel: 071 235 5454
Training department provides information suitable for health professionals and for the public.

RoSPA (Royal Society for the Prevention of Accidents)
Cannon House
Priory Queensway
Birmingham B4 6BS
Tel: 021 200 2461
Supplies a range of posters and leaflets suitable for the public.

British Safety Council
70 Chancellors Road
London W6 9RS
Tel: 081 741 1231

4 Resources

This chapter gives general information on where to obtain materials for health promotion.

Inclusion in this list does not imply recommendation by the Health Education Authority. Therefore, it is essential that you preview all material before use to check that it is appropriate, that it contains accurate up-to-date information in line with current medical thinking and that it is not invalidated by overt or covert advertising.

Leaflets

The Pharmacy Healthcare Scheme
The scheme sends leaflets on chosen topics to all pharmacies in the UK every few weeks. You can obtain further copies of some leaflets from the Pharmacy Healthcare Scheme, Royal Pharmaceutical Society.
Tel: 071 735 9141

You may also wish to display leaflets relating to other topics or need access to leaflets on a particular topic at times of year other than the Pharmacy Healthcare Scheme mailing (for instance on smoking cessation at a time other than around national No Smoking Day). The following sources may be helpful.

The Health Education Authority
The HEA produces a wide range of excellent leaflets. You may be able to obtain copies from your local health promotion unit or family health services authority. Alternatively, you can contact the HEA's customer services department, who will be able to give you details of these and other publications and how to order them at a nominal cost.
Tel: 071 383 3833

The HEA's Health Promotion Information Centre (HPIC) houses the largest collection of health promotion materials in the UK. In addition to a library and an audio-visual and teaching materials review collection,

HPIC publishes resource lists of material currently available on particular subjects or for specific target audiences.
Tel: 071 413 1995

Pharmaceutical wholesalers
Some pharmaceutical wholesalers are now supplying leaflets on selected health topics to their customers.

Self-help groups
Produce many useful leaflets. You will have received a copy of the *Self-help directory* from the Royal Pharmaceutical Society in April 1993. Please contact individual groups by writing (including stamped-addressed envelopes).

Department of Health
Customer leaflets are available from Department of Health Stores, No. 2 Site, Heywood Stores, Manchester Road, Heywood, Lancs OL10 2PZ.

Topics include:

Health advice for travellers – leaflets/dispenser/poster
HIV and AIDS leaflets
HIV, AIDS and drug use – leaflets (for parents and young people)
Solvent abuse leaflets
Drug abuse – leaflets/posters
Food safety – leaflet (various languages)
Tar and nicotine yield of cigarettes – leaflets and posters
Women's health – booklet
Children Act – booklets for parents and for young people
Health and healthy living for older people – booklet (various languages)
Breast awareness
Reducing the risk of cot death (various languages)
While you are pregnant – booklet (various languages)
The health of the nation booklet (summary)
The liquid medicine measure (oral syringe) – leaflet, (various languages)
Blood transfusion service – posters/leaflets
Organ donation cards/leaflets
Equipment and services for handicapped living – leaflets

The NPA Press Office
Keeps a selection of leaflets on various topics.
Tel: 0727 832161

The NPA Information Department
May be able to give details of suppliers of leaflets on specific topics.
Tel: 0727 832161

The Patient Support Trust
Provides a selection of leaflets for an administration fee (expected to be around £20 start-up fee, plus £2 postage and packaging per subsequent order).
Tel: 0489 891482

Pharmaceutical companies
Try them for leaflets on topics relating to the medicines they produce, for example:

Menopause	Companies producing HRT
Coronary heart disease	Manufacturers of cholesterol-lowering medicines, or antihypertensives
Smoking cessation	Manufacturers of nicotine replacement products

Always check commercial leaflets to ensure that health messages are not biased.

Videos and slide/lectures

The Royal Pharmaceutical Society
Has a wide range of videos/slides available. The service is offered free to all pharmacists in the United Kingdom. Loans are for up to two weeks. Contact: the Audio-visual Service, Room 403, Royal Pharmaceutical Society, 1 Lambeth High Street, London SE1 7JN. Tel: 071 735 9141, extension 288. A booklet giving full details of the lectures will be sent on request.

Local health promotion units
Most health promotion units have a library of videos which can be loaned free for a limited period, usually a week or two. Ask for a catalogue which will include a list of titles. Some units will deliver and collect these returnable items.

Family health services authorities

Some FHSAs now have video libraries providing free loans.

Other

- Videos are often available from self-help groups and from pharmaceutical manufacturers associated with specific illnesses/therapies. A list of current videos appears on pages 78–83, together with their sources.

- Note that videos on health subjects for pharmacists to stock and sell to customers are available from Video Collection International Ltd. Tel: 0923 255558

- Some videos are available free on loan to NPA members from the NPA Press Office. Tel: (0727) 832161

Always check that you have obtained the copyright owner's permission before showing any of these videos in your pharmacy (see page 15).

Books

- *Health promotion for pharmacists* (£8.95)
  Explains health promotion from the community pharmacist's point of view. It gives practical suggestions about drug misuse, family planning, baby and child health, and screening and diagnostic screening.
  NPA Sales Office. Tel: 0727 832161

- *Patient care in community practice* (£10)
  A guide to the background, use and range of non-medicinal products and appliances which may be used in the home.
  Pharmaceutical Press. Tel: 071 735 9141

- *Handbook of pharmacy health education* (£35)
  Intended to provide the pharmacist with background information to the aims of health education and looks at specific areas in which pharmacists may wish to become involved.
  Pharmaceutical Press. Tel: 071 735 9141

- *Training for health education: handbook* (£25.95)
  Ideas and suggestions for workshop activities, training exercises and handouts for use by tutors and others involved in health education training.
  Health Education Authority. Tel: 071 383 3833

Note that books on specific topics such as coronary heart disease prevention and cancer awareness are also available from the HEA. Tel: 071 383 3833

- *Diabetes – a guide for pharmacists (information pack)*
  Pharmacy Healthcare Scheme, Royal Pharmaceutical Society.
  Tel: 071 735 9141

- *Travellers' health – how to stay healthy abroad* (£5.99)
  Suitable for use by the pharmacist or to sell to patients.
  NPA Sales Office. Tel: 0727 832161

- *Better living – better life* (£15)
  A document aimed at all members of the primary healthcare team, looking at ways of preventing coronary heart disease. It was produced after a joint initiative between the Department of Health, the General Medical Services Council and the British Medical Association. It may provide useful background reading for pharmacists.
  Knowledge House Ltd, 13 Fairmile, Henley-on-Thames, Oxon RG9 2JR.

- *Cholesterol screening in community pharmacies*
  Overview of the role of cholesterol in CHD and the contribution that pharmacists can make. Free to NPA members or £5 to non-members.
  NPA Information Department. Tel: 0727 832161

- *Health promotion and health screening*
  A distance learning pack for pharmacists which contains general background information on health promotion as well as ideas for health screening in the pharmacy.
  Centre for Pharmacy Postgraduate Education. Tel: 061 275 2324

Table 1: Videos for specific illnesses/therapies

Subject	Video/title	Aimed at	Cost*	Contact	Comments
Arthritis	*Help is at hand*	Patients	£4.95 inc. p&p	Arthritis and Rheumatism Council Communications Tel: 0636 73054	
Asthma	*Away with the wheeze*	Patients/parents	Loaned free	RPSGB Audio-Visual Service Tel: 071 735 9141	
Asthma	*Managing your asthma*	Patients/parents	£5.00 each	National Asthma Campaign Tel: 071 226 2260	On childhood asthma
Back pain	*A new approach to an old problem*	Health professionals	Loaned free	NPA Press Office Tel: 0727 832161	Five Asian languages available only; not in English
Contraception	*Contraception – know what you are doing*	Public/teenagers	Loaned free	NPA Press Office Tel: 0727 832161	

Cystitis	*Overcoming cystitis*	Sufferers	£10.99 inc. p&p	Kilmartin Video Ltd PO Box 217 Walton on Thames Surrey KT12 3YF	Self-help techniques
Diabetes	Six videos on living with diabetes	Patients/parents	£9.99 inc. p&p	British Diabetic Association Tel: 071 323 1531	
Diabetes	*Treating hypoglycaemia*	Diabetic patients and their families and health professionals	Loaned free	NPA Press Office Tel: 0727 832161	
Drug use	Range of videos	Parents and retailers/health professionals	Various prices	Re-Solv Tel: 0785 817885	Contact Re-Solv for list
Drug use	*Right to care*	Pharmacists/GPs	Loaned free	Local FHSAs	Shows how to improve the healthcare offered to drug users and reduce the spread of HIV/AIDS

*as at October 1993

Table 1: Videos for specific illnesses/therapies – *continued*

Subject	Video/title	Aimed at	Cost*	Contact	Comments
Exercise	*Exercise: is it worth the effort?*	Pharmacists/GPs	Loaned free	NPA Press Office Tel: 0727 831161	
Exercise	*It doesn't have to hurt*	Public	£21.95 plus p&p	Health Education Authority	
Gastro-intestinal tract problems	*Living with inflammatory bowel disease*	Patients	Loaned free	NPA Press Office Tel: 0727 832161	
Gastro-intestinal tract problems	*Living with ulcerative colitis*	Patients	Free	Kabi Pharmacia Tel: 0908 661101	Pharmacist must obtain on patient's behalf
Gastro-intestinal tract problems	*The experience of ulcerative colitis*	Patients	Free	Smithkline Beecham Pharmaceuticals Tel: 0707 325111	Pharmacist must obtain on patient's behalf
Hay fever	*Hay fever – a western disease?*	Health professionals		Marion Merrell Dow Tel: 081 848 3456 or from reps	

Head lice	Let's lose lice	Parents	Loaned free	NPA Press Office Tel: 0727 832161	
Heart disease	Coronary artery disease – reducing the risk	Public	Loaned free	NPA Press Office Tel: 0727 832161	
Heart disease	Exercise your heart video – cardiovascular workout	Public	Free	Astra Pharmaceuticals Ltd Tel: 0923 266191	Supplied through pharmacies on request
Hypertension	Blood pressure measurement	Pharmacists/GPs	£24.95	British Medical Association Tel: 071 387 4499	
Hypertension	Modern management of essential hypertension	Pharmacists/GPs	Loaned free	NPA Press Office Tel: 0727 832161	Produced by the British Hypertension Society
Incontinence	Management of stress incontinence in women	Women	Free	Colgate Medical Tel: 0753 860378	

* as at October 1993

Table 1: Videos for specific illnesses/therapies – *continued*

Subject	Video/title	Aimed at	Cost*	Contact	Comments
Phamacist's role	*Working for patients*	Public	£25.00	Lancashire FHSA Tel: 0772 704141	Available in English and five Asian languages. Describes the services of community pharmacists, GPs, dentists and opticians
Pregnancy and babycare	*Baby quiz*	Parents-to-be or those with babies	£9.00	NPA Press Office Tel: 0727 832161	
Safe use of medicines		Public	Loaned free	NPA Training Dept Tel: 0727 832161	Suitable for pharmacists providing services to residential homes and training care staff, and home helps. Suitable also for talks to women's groups

Sickle Cell	*Let's talk sickle*	People affected by sickle cell	£19.99	Sickle Cell Society Tel: 081 961 7795	Available in six Asian languages only. Not available in English
Thalassaemia	*What is thalassaemia?*	People affected by thalassaemia	£25.00	UK Thalassaemia Society Tel: 081 348 0437	
Toxoplasmosis	Video in two parts	First part – pregnant women Second part – health professionals	£9.00 inc. p&p	Toxoplasmosis Trust Tel: 071 713 0599	First part explains how to avoid infection. Second part contains more technical information for health professionals
Various	Videos on health subjects including asthma, skin problems, heart problems, etc.	Public		Video Collection International Ltd Tel: 0923 255558	Available for pharmacists to sell to customers

*as at October 1993

5 Suppliers of diagnostic equipment

Pregnancy tests

Lists of suppliers of professional and home pregnancy tests are given in Tables 2 and 3 (pages 88–93; phone numbers pages 91 and 93).

Weighing machines

Coin-in-Slot
Vandoni, Anglo European Health. Tel: 061 766 2313
Weylux 'Healthweigh', H Fereday & Sons Ltd. Tel: 071 607 5601
Both machines are available through NPA Sales Office. Tel: 0727 832161

'Beam' type
Albert Browne Ltd. Tel: 0533 340730
W & T Avery Ltd. Tel: 0622 671370
H Fereday & Sons Ltd. Tel: 071 607 5601
Marsden Weighing Machine Group. Tel: 071 289 1066
Seca Ltd. Tel: 021 643 9349
Timesco of London. Tel: 071 278 0712

Cholesterol screening equipment and services

The NPA publication, *Cholesterol screening in community pharmacies*, gives useful background information if you wish to set up a screening service.

For professional use

Accumeter*   Anglo European Health. Tel: 061 766 2313
Lipotrend C Boehringer Mannheim Diagnostics Ltd. Tel: 0273 480444
Minilab   Bayer Diagnostics UK Ltd. Tel: 0256 29181 (can also test
             for other substances)

Quik Read*   Anglo European Health. Tel: 061 766 2313
Reflotron   Boehringer Mannheim Diagnostics Ltd. Tel: 0273 480444
              (can also test for other substances)
Chemachol   Lifeline UK. Tel: 0904 488958
              (Note that the reagent kit used with this machine can also
              be used satisfactorily with the Cholestratest equipment
              which is now discontinued.)

* These machines are also available through the NPA Sales Office.
  Tel: 0727 832161

For home use (for public to purchase)

Chemcard   Farillon Ltd. Tel: 0708 379000
Clinimeter   Anglo European Health. Tel: 061 766 2313
Boots   From Boots pharmacies only

Note that the HEA does not support home or self-testing of cholesterol levels.

Computer programs

Cholesterol, urine and blood pressure readings are fed into the computer
with other patient details. The program then produces a computerised
health screening report for the customer.
Takeheart Health Check. Tel: 0603 54314

Pharmacheck

Provided by Pharmaforce. The owner of the business provides shop space
for testing and Pharmaforce provide another pharmacist to carry out the
testing. The customer is charged for the cholesterol test and an appropriate percentage goes to the owner of the business and to the pharmacist
and/or company providing the service.
Tel: 0257 232518

Primetest

Available from Unichem. It is an integrated system producing an overall risk assessment of cardiovascular disease, and measures blood glucose and blood cholesterol as well as blood pressure. Other risk factors are keyed into the system which then produces a risk assessment figure and prints out results.

Unichem. Tel: 081 391 2323

Blood glucose meters

A list of suppliers of blood glucose meters is given in Table 4 (page 94; phone numbers page 95).

Blood pressure

A list of suppliers of blood pressure monitoring equipment is given in Table 5 (page 96; phone numbers page 97).

Table 2: Suppliers of professional pregnancy tests

Product	Manufacturer	Form	Used from	Time	Positive result
Aura Tek	Organon Teknika	Chromotographic	2–5 days before expected period	4 min	Color change in window
Beta hCG	Roche	Slide	1st day of missed period	2 min	No agglutination
Pregnancy Slide	Roche	Slide	12 days after missed period	2 min	No agglutination
Card OS hCG	BHR Pharmaceuticals	Sample unit	1st day of missed period	5 min	Blue positive sign in window
Clearview	Unipath	Absorbent pad	1st day of missed period	5 min	Blue line in result window
Concise	BHR Pharmaceuticals	Sample well	10 days after conception	5 min	Two bars in window

Product	Supplier	Sample unit	Timing	Time	Positive sign
Early Bird Haxagon hCG	Kent Pharmaceuticals	Hexagon disc	5 days before missed period	2 min	
Event	Boehringer Mannheim Diagnostics	Tube	6–10 days after missed period	1 hour	Coloured ring appears in tube
Gravindex beta hCG	Ortho Diagnostics	Slide	1–5 days after missed period	2 min	No agglutination
hCG-Nostick	Organon Teknika	Dipstick	1st day after missed period	5 min	White to purple colour change
Neo Planotest Duoclon	Organon Teknika	Slide	4–6 days after missed period	2 min	Agglutination
Neo Planotest 200	Organon Teknika	Slide	2–4 days after missed period	2 min	Agglutination
Pregna Sure hCG	Merlin Pharmaceuticals	Sample unit	2 days after missed period	3 min	Positive sign in window
Pregnospia Duoclon	Organon Teknika	Tube	3 days after missed period	4–5 min	Magenta to clear colour change

Table 2: Suppliers of professional pregnancy tests – *continued*

Product	Manufacturer	Form	Used from	Time	Positive result
Pregnosticon All-In	Organon Teknika	Tube	10 days after missed period	1 hour	Firm button of cells at bottom of tube
Pregstik	Organon Laboratories	Dipstick	1 day before period due	30 min	Red colour on stick
Quick Vue	Medimar	Dipstick	10 days after conception	3 min	Red line in window
RAMP	Medimar	Rapid absorbent matrix pad	10 days after conception	3–4 min	Blue dot
Tandem Icon	Britpharm Laboratories	Cylinder with permeable membrane	1st day of missed period	3–4 min	Blue dot
Test Pack Plus	Abbott Laboratories	Disc	14 days after conception	2–3 min	Positive sign in window

Phone numbers of suppliers

Abbott Laboratories Ltd	Tel: 0628 773355
BHR Pharmaceuticals Ltd	Tel: 0203 353742
Boehringer Mannheim Diagnostics	Tel: 0273 480444
Britpharm Laboratories Ltd	Tel: 071 370 0403
Kent Pharmaceuticals Ltd	Tel: 0233 641802
Medimar Laboratories	Tel: 0865 874110
Merlin Pharmaceuticals Ltd	Tel: 081 311 9461
Organon Laboratories	Tel: 0223 423445
Organon Teknika	Tel: 0223 423650
Ortho Diagnostics	Tel: 0494 442211
Roche	Tel: 0707 366000
Unipath	Tel: 0234 347161

Table 3: Suppliers of home pregnancy tests

Product	Manufacturer	Used from	Procedure	Time	Positive result	Other details
Clearblue One Step	Unipath	1st day of missed period	Hold test in urine stream	3 min	Blue line in result window	Single or double test
Conceive	Medimar Labs	1st day of missed period	Add 3 drops of urine to sample sample pad	1–3 min	Red line in window	Single or double test
Discover Today	Carter Wallace	1st day of missed period	Hold test in urine stream	3 min	Pink line in window	Single or double test
Early Bird	Kent Pharmaceuticals	1st day of missed period	Hold test in urine stream	5 min	Positive or negative sign	Single test
First response	Carter Wallace	1st day of missed period	Hold test in urine stream	5 min	Pink to purple colour	Single or double test
Precise	Becton Dickinson	1st day of missed period	Put urine into a well in test device	1 min	Blue tick	Single or double test
Predictor	Chefaro	1st day of missed period	Dip test in urine for five seconds	4 min	Colour change	Single or double test

Phone numbers of suppliers

Becton Dickinson	Tel: 0865 748844
Carter Wallace	Tel: 0303 850661
Chefaro	Tel: 0223 420956
Kent Pharmaceuticals	Tel: 0233 641802
Medimar Laboratories	Tel: 0865 874110
Unipath	Tel: 0234 347161

Table 4: Suppliers of blood glucose meters

Blood glucose meter		Blood glucose testing strip							
Meter	Manufacturer	BM Test 1–44	Glucostix	Hypoguard GA	Hypoguard Supreme	Exac-Tech	BM Accutest	Medi-Test Glucose	One Touch
Glucometer GX/II	Bayer Diagnostics		✓						
Reflolux S	Boehringer Mannheim Diagnostics	✓							
ExacTech	Medisense Britain					✓			
HypoCount GA	Hypoguard UK			✓					
HypoCount Supreme	Hypoguard UK				✓				
Accutrend	Boehringer Mannheim Diagnostics						✓		
Glycotronic C	BHR Pharmaceuticals							✓	
One Touch II/Basic	Lifescan								✓

Note that most strips can be read visually but some patients/pharmacists prefer to use meters.

Phone numbers of suppliers

Bayer Diagnostics UK Ltd   Tel: 0256 29181
BHR Pharmaceuticals   Tel: 0203 353742
Boehringer Mannheim Diagnostics   Tel: 0273 480444
Hypoguard (UK) Ltd   Tel: 0394 387333
Lifescan   Tel: 0494 442211
Medisense Britain Ltd   Tel: 0675 467044

Table 5: Suppliers of blood pressure monitoring equipment and pulse meters

Type of equipment	Suppliers (see below)
Aneroid (manual dial)	3, 6, 8, 10, 11, 12, 14, 15, 16, 17, 19, 23, 24, 25, 26, 28
Mercury	3, 6, 8, 9, 10, 11, 14, 15, 16, 19, 23, 24, 26
Digital with printer	1, 4, 5, 13, 18, 19, 20, 21, 22, 24, 25, 28
without printer	1, 2, 5, 12, 13, 14, 15, 16, 17, 19, 20, 22, 25, 26, 27
finger cuff	1, 5, 12, 13, 15, 19, 21, 25, 27
Shop use	1, 20
Shop-use: coin-operated	7
Pulse meter	5, 13, 15, 16, 22, 28
Pulse meter: watch-type	12, 24

Phone numbers of suppliers

1	A and D Instruments	Tel: 0235 550420
2	AAH Pharmaceuticals Ltd	Tel: 0928 717070
3	Albert Browne Ltd	Tel: 0533 340730
4	Anglo European Health	Tel: 061 766 2313
5	Bodycare Products Ltd	Tel: 0926 50935
6	Browning Medical	Tel: 081 805 7575
7	Checkmate Servicing	Tel: 0582 842319
8	A J Cope and Son Ltd	Tel: 071 729 2405
9	A C Cossor and Son Ltd	Tel: 081 800 1172
10	East Healthcare Ltd	Tel: 0865 714242
11	Engstrom MIE	Tel: 0392 431331
12	Fisons Scientific	Tel: 0509 231166
13	Hutchings Healthcare Ltd	Tel: 0273 495034
14	Keeler Ltd	Tel: 0753 857177
15	Medipost UK Ltd	Tel: 0305 760750
16	Pan Servico Surgical Ltd	Tel: 081 764 1806
17	Philip Harris Medical	Tel: 021 433 3030
18	Philips Electronics	Tel: 081 689 2166
19	Porter Nash	Tel: 071 486 1434
20	Schuco International Ltd	Tel: 081 368 1642
21	Selfcare Products Ltd	Tel: 0494 722741
22	Selles Medical Ltd	Tel: 0482 659485
23	Shermond Surgical Supply Ltd	Tel: 0273 588577
24	Surgicon Ltd	Tel: 0484 712147
25	Timesco of London	Tel: 071 278 0712
26	TVM Healthcare	Tel: 0530 565100
27	Voltastar	Tel: 0235 550420
28	Waeschle	Tel: 0202 290502

Appendix: Important dates for 1994

Date(s)	Event	Contact
All year	International Year of the Family	Veronica Ashworth International Year of the Family, 1994 Yalding House 152 Great Portland Street London W1N 6AJ Tel: 071 637 2755
9 March	No Smoking Day	Clare Duke Health Education Authority Tel: 071 413 1996
13–19 March	National Continence Awareness Week	Continence Foundation 2 Doughty Street London WC1N 2PH Tel: 071 404 6875
7 April	World Health Day (Theme: Oral Health)	World Health Organization Avenue Appia CH-1211 Geneva 27 Switzerland Tel: 010 41 22 791 2111
16–24 April	Cystic Fibrosis Week	Cystic Fibrosis Research Trust Alexandra House 5 Blyth Road Bromley Kent BR1 3RS Tel: 081 464 7211
May	Enjoy Fruit & Veg Month	Mary Robinson Health Education Authority Tel: 071 413 1830

Date(s)	Event	Contact
9–15 May	Adult Learners' Week	National Institute of Adult Continuing Education 19b De Montfort Street Leicester LE1 7GE Tel: 0533 551451
16–22 May	National Smile Week	British Dental Health Foundation Eastlands Court St Peter's Road Rugby Warwick CV21 3QP Tel: 0788 546365
16–22 May	Epilepsy Week	National Society for Epilepsy Chalfont Centre for Epilepsy Chalfont St Peter Gerrards Cross Bucks SL9 0RJ Tel: 0494 873991
31 May	World No Tobacco Day	World Health Organization Avenue Appia CH-1211 Geneva 27 Switzerland Tel: 010 41 22 791 2111
6–11 June	National Food Safety Week	External Relations Division Food and Drink Federation 6 Catherine Street London WC2B 5JJ Tel: 071 836 2460 x2235/6
12–19 June	Defeat Diabetes Week	British Diabetic Association 10 Queen Anne Street London W1M 0BD Tel: 071 323 1531 Fax: 071 636 3096
14 June	Drinkwise Day	Sarah Harris Health Education Authority Tel: 071 413 1818
26 June–2 July	Psoriasis Awareness Week	The Psoriasis Association Milton House 7 Milton Street Northampton NN2 7JG Tel: 0604 711129 Fax: 0604 792894

Date(s)	Event	Contact
1–7 July	Child Safety Week	Child Accident Prevention Trust 4th Floor, Clerks Court 18–20 Farringdon Lane London EC1R 3AU Tel: 071 608 3828 Fax: 071 608 3674
4–9 July	Alzheimer's Disease Awareness Week	Alzheimer's Disease Society 158–60 Balham High Road London SW12 9BW Tel: 071 306 0606
8–15 August	National Condom Week	British Safety Council 70 Chancellors Road London W6 9RS Tel: 081 741 1231
5–11 September	National Migraine Week	Migraine Trust 45 Great Ormond Street London WC1N 3HZ Tel: 071 278 2676
11–17 September	Imperial Cancer Week	Imperial Cancer Research Fund 61 Lincolns Inn Fields London WC2A 3PX Tel: 071 269 3413
17–24 September	Arthritis Care Week	Arthritis Care 18 Stephenson Way London NW1 2HD Tel: 071 916 1500
1–8 October	National Eczema Week	National Eczema Society 4 Tavistock Place London WC1H 9RA Tel: 071 388 4097 Fax: 071 713 0733
3–10 October	National Stroke Week	The Stroke Association CHSA House Whitecross Street London EC1Y 8JJ Tel: 071 490 7999 Fax: 071 490 2686

Date(s)	Event	Contact
8–15 October	Foot Health Week	The Foot Health Council c/o Wessex School of Podiatry Department F 7 Archers Road Southampton SO1 2LQ
10–15 October	National Back Pain Week	National Back Pain Association 31–33 Park Road Teddington Middlesex TW11 0AB Tel: 081 977 5474
10–16 October	Asthma Week	National Asthma Campaign Providence House Providence Place London N1 0NT Tel: 071 226 2260
10–16 October	Europe Against Cancer Week	Janet Marshall EEC Officer 8 Storey's Gate Jean Monet House London SW1P 3AT Tel: 071 973 1906
15–22 October	European Drug Prevention Week	Information Division Department of Health Skipton House 80 London Road Elephant and Castle London SE1 6LW Tel: 071 972 6541 Freephone: 0800 555 777
17–23 October	National Vegetarian Week	Vegetarian Society Parkdale Durham Road Altrincham Cheshire WA14 4QG Tel: 061 928 0793
31 October	Bug Busters Day (headlice)	Community Hygiene Concern 32 Crane Avenue Isleworth Middlesex Tel: 081 341 7167

Date(s)	Event	Contact
1 December	World AIDS Day (Theme: The Family)	National Aids Trust Eileen House 80 Newington Causeway London SE1 6EF Tel: 071 972 2845
3 December	International Day of Disabled Persons	Disability Awareness in Action 11 Belgrave Road London SW1V 1RB Tel: 071 834 0477 Fax: 071 821 9539
4–11 December	National Autism Week	National Autistic Society 276 Willesden Lane London NW2 5RB Tel: 081 451 1114

Health promotion contacts

	Name
Health promotion officer	
Health promotion unit	
FHSA facilitator/health promotion officer	
General practitioners	
Practice nurses	
District dietitian	
Health visitor	
Community nurses	
Dentists	
Environmental health officer	
Press or media	
Other	

Address and telephone